ADVANCE PRAISE FOR *A GLASS FULL OF MIRACLES*

~

"Mike Grgich may be small in stature, but he is a giant in the world of wine. His new book dramatically tells his full story, which is a great tale of a dream come true. I heard some of his stories when I was working on my book *Judgment of Paris*, and in reading his book I felt like I was listening to him tell them again. You hear the voice of Mike come through loud and clear. The book also shows that there are a lot more aspects to Mike's life than just Cabernet and Chardonnay. It's a great and fun read."

—George M. Taber, author of *Judgment of Paris*

"Anyone who has spent more than a few minutes with Napa Valley winemaker Mike Grgich knows that he loves to tell stories. This penchant for spinning tales, when combined with the incredibly long, storied life he has led, makes an engaging, almost lyrical memoir that's entertaining for the average person and compelling for the person who appreciates fine wine or modern history."

—Jim Gordon, Editor, *Wines & Vines*

Mike Grgich not only changed the course of the wine world at the Judgment of Paris 40 years ago, but the wines he made — and still makes — have always set a standard for other producers to emulate. Though many California winemakers have followed chic trends over the years, the standard has once again returned to the classic elegance Mike has always espoused. This book helps explain why.

—Paul Franson, Publisher of *NapaLife* and author of *The NapaLife Insider's Guide to Napa Valley*

"This would be an important oral history of one of Napa Valley's most famous winemakers even if it were dull. Fortunately, it's not. Mike Grgich's voice is personable and his brisk retelling of events puts you right there, whether he's losing his shirt in a river before an important boyhood religious ceremony, or hoping for the color to return to normal in an important Chardonnay. Mike has lived an amazing life and this book captures it."

—W. Blake Gray, wine columnist and publisher of *The Gray Report*

"His Old World gumption packed in a flimsy valise, diminutive Miljenko Grgich fled oppression in his native Croatia more than half a century ago to stand tall in the emerging California wine industry. His travails and triumphs are laid out by the 92-year-old vintner in an autobiographical page turner that wine enthusiasts all over the world will appreciate. I'm proud to have crossed paths with Mike Grgich and to call him a friend."

—Pierce Carson, Food/Arts/Wine Reporter, *Napa Register*

"The journey of Miljenko 'Mike' Grgich from his homeland, Croatia, to rock star status in California's Napa Valley is a gripping tale, made all the more inspiring by Mike's spectacular success as a winemaker. Grgich figured prominently in the dramatic rise of the Napa Valley as the man who made the legendary 1973 Chateau Montelena Chardonnay that triumphed at the famous Judgment of Paris tastings. He went on to even greater acclaim as winemaker/proprietor of Grgich Hills Cellars, an estate that now boasts more than 300 acres of planted vineyards. *A Glass Full of Miracles* is a remarkable story well told."

—Robert Whitley, publisher and managing partner of *Wine Review Online* and author of "Wine Talk," a column syndicated nationally by the Creators Syndicate.

"Even though Grgich is America's most influential winemaker, this book is more about life than wine. It has lessons for us all—and you needn't be a wine lover to enjoy it."

—Dr. Michael Apstein, Columnist, winereviewonline.com

"My wife Sheila and I have been great friends with Mike Grgich from his early days at Chateau Montelena in the 1970's. We were delighted and enjoyed reading his biography of his family and background in this book. It was my privilege to have sponsored Mike to become a Supreme Knight in the SF Bay Area chapter of the Brotherhood of Knights of the Vine. He joined with other California great Supreme Knights such as Robert Mondavi, Julio Gallo, Joseph Heitz, Warren Winiarski, and Andre Tchelistcheff in this honor. The KOV is a member of the International Wine Brotherhoods of the World, FICB."

—Dr. Ron Light, Master Vice Commander,
San Francisco Bay Chapter of the Knights of the Vine

A Glass Full *of* Miracles

A Glass Full *of* Miracles

Miljenko "Mike" Grgich

445 E. 1st Street
Napa, California 94559
www.violettapress.com
violettapress@gmail.com

© Copyright 2016 by Violetta Press
ALL RIGHTS RESERVED

No part of this book may be reproduced by any means whatsoever without written permission from the publisher except brief portions quoted for purpose of review.

First Edition

ISBN: 978-0-692-60120-4
Library of Congress Control Number: 2016902173

I DEDICATE THIS BOOK TO THE MEMORY OF MY PARENTS,

IVKA AND NIKOLA GRGIĆ,

FROM WHOM I LEARNED THE BEST VALUES IN LIFE.

I ALSO DEDICATE IT TO MY TEN BROTHERS AND SISTERS,

WHO HAVE JOINED OUR PARENTS IN HEAVEN.

IVKA AND NIKOLA GRGIĆ

Acknowledgments

I HAD JUST TURNED 90 YEARS OLD and my daughter Violet was urging me to write my memoirs. The decision was not easy. However, with much encouragement and the promise of support, I faced the challenge and would like to thank the people who assisted me in writing this book.

To Sasha Paulsen, a journalist in Napa Valley, who came to my home to record my thoughts, transcribed the tapes and was instrumental in making what was just a concept become a reality — compiling the accomplishments of my life into this book, *A Glass Full of Miracles*.

Many thanks to my friend Maria Luisa Moreno Reyes, who spent countless hours helping me write down my memories, doing research, and typing and retyping the draft of the book. She burned the midnight oil until we concluded the manuscript.

To Ariel Jackson, Sasha Paulsen's daughter and a graduate of the University of California, Davis, with a Masters Degree in Linguistics, who was a great help in reviewing the manuscript and suggesting changes.

To Steven Spurrier, who, in collaboration with his associate Patricia Gallagher, was the 'brains' behind the 1976 wine competition of the best French wines vs. the little-known California wines. This event gave me the opportunity to prove that we could make wine not only as good as the French, but better than the French.

To George Taber, who, as the only eyewitness and journalist present in the room at the InterContinental Hotel in Paris at the time, chronicled the now historic 1976 Paris Tasting. I thank him for allowing us to use excerpts from his book, *The Judgment of Paris*.

I also wish to acknowledge the support of Mr. Theodore Kolb, my lawyer and friend throughout the years until his death in March 2015.

To my good partners Mary Lee Strebl and Austin Hills, my nephew Ivo Jeramaz, my loyal staff at Grgich Hills and the many others I have not been able to mention — thank you.

Most of all, I would like to thank my daughter Violet for urging me to write down my achievements and keeping after me until I had done it.

Table of Contents

ACKNOWLEDGMENTS		
INTRODUCTION BY ZELMA LONG		3
PROLOGUE		9
CHAPTER 1:	A Shepherd from Desne	15
CHAPTER 2:	A Young Student	29
CHAPTER 3:	War	39
CHAPTER 4:	The Communists Take Power	53
CHAPTER 5:	To Zagreb	63
CHAPTER 6:	Escape	75
PHOTOGRAPHS PART ONE:	Youth and Early Influences	87
CHAPTER 7:	The New World	105
CHAPTER 8:	Finally Paradise!	117
CHAPTER 9:	The Christian Brothers	131
CHAPTER 10:	André Tchelistcheff	145
PHOTOGRAPHS PART TWO:	Putting Down Roots	169
CHAPTER 11:	Robert Mondavi	179

CHAPTER 12:	Chateau Montelena	199
CHAPTER 13:	The Judgment of Paris	227
CHAPTER 14:	The Founding of Grgich Hills	243
PHOTOGRAPHS PART THREE:	Passion for Success	261
CHAPTER 15:	The King of Chardonnay	277
CHAPTER 16:	A String of Pearls	295
CHAPTER 17:	Return to Croatia	311
CHAPTER 18:	Grgić Vina	319
CHAPTER 19:	The Mystery of Zinfandel	333
CHAPTER 20:	The Roots of Peace	345
CHAPTER 21:	Like the Old Vines	355
CHAPTER 22:	The Perfect Wine	367
PHOTOGRAPHS PART FOUR:	A Multitude of Harvests	375
CHAPTER 23:	Miracles	403
PHOTO CREDITS:		411

A Glass Full *of* Miracles

Introduction

A REMARKABLE MAN, AN EXTRAORDINARY LIFE: THIS IS MIKE GRGICH.

An immigrant from Croatia, he arrived in California in 1958 and began his Napa Valley career in wine. Over time, he was recognized and awarded for his winemaking talent and his special touch with Chardonnay. In 1976, his 1973 Chateau Montelena Chardonnay won the tasting referred to as "The Judgment of Paris", besting great French estate Chardonnays in a blind tasting judged by the wine experts of France. His Chardonnay became an icon of Napa Valley excellence; his victory created a "tipping point" for Napa Valley and indeed the New World of wines. After that, Napa and California wines emerged from being considered "amusing curiosities" by traditional European wine lovers and wine media, to wines worthy of note, and in time, recognized as among the greatest wines of the world.

Mike was raised with grapes and wine; his Croatian family farmed their own grapes and made their own wine. Almost

⁓ Miljenko "Mike" Grgich

since he was old enough to walk, he had been in his family's vineyard. When at age fifty-six he and his partners opened their Napa winery, Grgich Hills, he noted that he already had 47 years of experience with grapes and wine. Even after many decades as an American citizen he still feels rooted in Croatia, and thirty-six years after departing his homeland, he was able to return and start his own winery in Dalmatia, the coastal region of his birth. He was delighted when the mysterious origins of California's iconic grape, Zinfandel, were unraveled in 2000, and were found to be the grape Crljenak Kaštelanski, a native Croatian grape. It had arrived in the U.S. in the 1800s, a grape immigrant without an identified name. Mike's home vineyard in the Napa Valley outside of Calistoga grows his well-loved Zinfandel vines.

I met Mike in 1970, when he approached me to take a break from my UC Davis enology studies to work with him as a harvest intern at Robert Mondavi Winery. The internship evolved into a full time position and a chance to learn from him. Mike was a natural storyteller, illustrating his sensory observations and winemaking work, imprinting them into my winemaking life. I believe that Mike's combination of professional knowledge and passionate devotion to wine has made him the great winemaker that he is.

Mike was educated and trained in enology and viticulture in Croatia, where he studied the technical aspects of grapes and wine. Assisting André Tchelistcheff at Beaulieu he expanded his technical expertise, and has continued to use his professional training to understand wine. But the Mike I remember brought more to wine than just his training. He loved wine: it was his passion. He was connected to his wines: they were his children, he raised them, he touched them, he cared for them. He did not position himself as the "master" of the wines; or as the wine "expert"; instead, he was a father and mother to them, deeply observant, sensitive, and caring. It was this European sensibility, observed in my wine travels to France and Italy, that led me to understand Mike's profound connection to his wines, which has given his wines their special beauty.

Young winemakers today express the desire to "raise" their wines: to touch and handle them, to be gentle, to express the vineyard site and the grape DNA. Although sometimes positioned as a "new direction" in winemaking, I first sensed and saw it in 1970 working with Mike. All winemakers can do well to emulate his relationship with his vines and the systematic time he spends in his vineyards.

Mike's story adds significantly to the history of the formative years of Napa Valley's wine renaissance of the 1970s and 1980s. His California wine career intersected with many of the early "greats" of Napa Valley wine, including Lee Stewart of Souverain, André Tchelistcheff of Beaulieu, and of course, Robert Mondavi. I believe that an important historical contribution to current and future winemakers is the detailed description of the specific winemaking process and grape sources he used for his famed 1973 Chateau Montelena Chardonnay.

His numerous historic achievements in wine might lead readers to expect that his story would merely reflect his wine education and practice. Yet he has written on a much broader palette, that of the whole of his life, from its solid family

∞ Miljenko "Mike" Grgich

foundation and the deep strength thus generated to his long, determined, and persistent journey to a California life in wine, with many unexpected and wonderful consequences of his open thinking, warm and loyal heart, bright mind, and clear sense of values. His is the story of a life well and fully lived.

— Zelma Long
September 2015

Zelma Long

My passport picture, 1954

Prologue

It was the summer of 1954. Although the day was warm, I felt ice cold as I sat on the train that was charging toward the border of Yugoslavia. When it slowed to a halt, my heart was pounding as loud as the engines. The guards appeared: stern-faced men with guns, watching people who got off to pass through the border controls. The inspectors would check everyone trying to leave Yugoslavia; one false step and you would not be getting back on the train.

My papers were in order, stating that I, Miljenko Grgić, was a student from the University of Zagreb in Croatia, which was then a part of communist Yugoslavia. I had been granted a four-month passport to take part in a United Nations student exchange. I was being allowed to leave Yugoslavia to work the harvest in Germany.

The guards inspected the things I was carrying. A little cardboard suitcase held all I owned in the world; most important to me were my fifteen textbooks on winemaking. I wondered if they were going to ask me why I was wearing a

French beret. Would they believe me if I told the truth: I had lost my umbrella and this was the cheapest covering for my head that I, a poor student, had been able to afford?

Let them ask me about my hat, I thought, as long as they don't look too closely at my shoes. There I had hidden another treasure, thirty-two American dollars. To carry foreign currency out of Yugoslavia was forbidden, as were many things under the rule of Communism. If they found it, the guards would not only confiscate my money but they would take my passport as well. Even if I didn't end up in prison, I would never get another passport, another chance to escape.

That is what I meant to do. If I got past the border, I was never coming back to this country, my homeland, dominated now by fear and oppression — where you never knew when the secret police might be following you; where people disappeared and you never saw them again; where you didn't know if you would be alive or dead the next day; where you had no chance to work for your dreams.

I had carefully collected my thirty-two American dollars, and somehow I was going to get to America, to a place I had only heard of in whispers: California. I wanted to own a piece of land I could call my own. I wanted to make wine. But most of all, I wanted to be free.

God was with me that day, as He often has been in my life. The inspector stamped my passport, I got back on the train, and then I began to breathe again.

Today, more than half a century later, when I think about that young man and his crazy plans I know that, as big as his dreams were, he never could have imagined what lay ahead. What would I have replied if someone had told me that I, a boy from the village of Desne, Croatia, would not only get to America but that one day my little suitcase, my winemaking books, and even my beret would have a place in the great Smithsonian Institution in Washington, D.C.? That one day I would own, not just a patch of land, but hundreds of acres and a winery that people would come to visit from all over the world? And that one day I would be able to return to my homeland, Croatia, to my friends and family that I was leaving behind? That I would even own a winery there too?

My beret, suitcase and textbooks in the Smithsonian Institution.

✤ Miljenko "Mike" Grgich

That would be a miracle, I would have said back in 1954. Today, many years later, I would say it was quite a few miracles that made all of this happen.

It was a long journey that began on that day in 1954 and brought me here, to my home in Calistoga in Napa Valley. I wonder, is it a coincidence that this, my last home, reminds me so much of my first home, thousands of miles away in Desne, Croatia? My house in Calistoga is on a hillside, like my family's house in Desne. Grapevines grow on the slope below the house, just as they did at my boyhood home. I have planted fruit trees, peaches, apricots and figs, along with a garden of tomatoes and zucchinis — the same things that my family ate long ago. I have also planted lavender, which is very popular in Croatia, and varieties of roses that thrive in Napa Valley as well as in Croatia.

Most of all it is the mountain that reminds me of Desne. In Calistoga, I look out at Mount St. Helena, the highest peak in Napa Valley; how much, for me, it resembles Babina Gomila, the mighty mountain that towers over Desne and where, as a boy, I took my sheep to graze.

I have climbed Mount St. Helena as many times as I climbed Babina Gomila in the old country. How do you climb a mountain? You go one step at a time. Even if sometimes you turn back, you return and try again until you have reached the top. They say only God can make a miracle, but I also think we help miracles to happen, by always moving forward, step by step, towards our dreams, by learning every day and remembering all we have learned. In other words, God may be in charge of miracles but we can help them along the way.

Now I have some time to think back on my life: on my humble beginnings, narrow escapes, and various successes. I am content because I have the four things that matter to me: God, family, friends — and wine. The events of the world have shaped my life in ways that I, who started out a poor shepherd on the peaceful slopes of Babina Gomila, could not have imagined. Many people in my life helped me achieve my dreams. I have had the good fortune to learn from outstanding teachers along the way. But the deepest-rooted lessons of my life come from my father and my mother. Today in Calistoga, I let my old Zinfandel vines grow the way my father did in his vineyards in Desne. The vines have just one stake to lean on if they need it. They are not tied up because vines, like people, have to be free.

— Mike Grgich
Calistoga, California, 2015

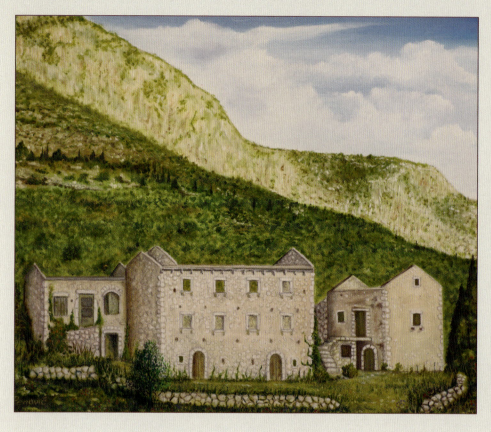

The house where I grew up.
It had no modern amenities but it was shelter and a home.

Chapter 1

A Shepherd from Desne

*I*N CROATIA, THE CUSTOM IS TO give a baby the name of a relative. When the new one is the youngest of eleven children, though, you begin to run out of family members to honor. But this is not the only reason I was named for the postman of Desne. It's true my parents needed a name, but this postman was also an important person for our family. Once a year he brought us a letter from America. It came from my oldest sister, Manda, who had gone to America before I was born and lived in Aberdeen, in the state of Washington. She had gotten married there to Vide Domandich, and was so prosperous that each Christmas she sent the family a five-dollar bill. That was the most money we would see all year.

My mother had thought about naming me after her father, George. St. George is the patron saint of Desne and the church of Sveti Jure (St. George) was built in his honor. So George was a logical choice. My mother worried, however, that her father had too many problems with his stomach, as did she, so my parents gave me the name of the postman, Miljenko, who delivered the five dollars to us each year at Christmas. Though this didn't prevent my own stomach problems, perhaps it began my ties to America.

Croatia is a tiny country that lies along the Adriatic Sea, across from Italy, in southern Europe. It is about the size of West Virginia, but its land includes more than a thousand islands scattered along its coastline.

It is an ancient country. The independent kingdom of Croatia was founded in 925, and lasted for two centuries until Croatia merged with Hungary, which in turn became part of the Austro-Hungarian Empire. It was part of this Empire when World War I began and my father, Nikola Grgić, left home to serve in the Austrian army for five years. During these long years, my mother, Ivka, had no word from him. She didn't know if he was dead or alive. She took care of their eight children and the farm all by herself.

How hard she must have worked, I cannot imagine, but she was a strong and smart woman. She never learned to read, but she knew how to live. She would send my brothers and sisters out every day to forage for food. Pomegranates grew wild, as did mulberry trees and asparagus. Uncle Marin taught us how to fish, and how to make traps to catch birds. The neighbors helped us, too, and so we survived.

When my father came home from the war, the Spanish flu also arrived in Desne. My mother and my brothers and sisters all got sick, and so the first thing he had to do was to care for his family. Two of my brothers and two sisters died of this flu.

The Austro-Hungarian Empire was dissolved at the end of the war, and when I was born on April 1, 1923, Croatia had become part of the Kingdom of Serbs, Croats and Slovenes. There was great hope that these three countries would be equals, but, in reality, the Serbs in their capital of Belgrade dominated. When some Croatians complained about this, the Serbians killed the Croatian leader, Stjepan Radić. On his deathbed he told the other Croatian leaders, "Never to Belgrade again!" But Croatia would not become an independent country again until 1991.

As part of the Kingdom, which was renamed Yugoslavia in 1929, Croatia was occupied during World War II first by Italian Fascists and then by German Nazis. After the war, it was part of Communist Yugoslavia. All of these world events shaped my life, even in a little place like Desne.

In my time, Desne was a village of about one thousand people on the west side of the River Neretva, which flows to the Adriatic Sea. Most of the old houses, like the one where I was born, were built high up above the river and lake for protection from the pirates who would come from the sea. Later, when the people did not have to worry about pirates, they built houses lower, at the base of the mountain, Babina Gomila.

The Grgić family had lived in Desne as long as anyone could remember. It was the custom that in a family, one of the children would remain in the village and live in the family home, while the others would go out to new places. This is how I had uncles in America.

∽ Miljenko "Mike" Grgich

My father was the Grgić who had stayed in Desne to raise a new family. When my grandfather, Mijo Grgić, passed away, my Uncle Marin overheard people say at the funeral, "What will happen to the Grgić family now that Mijo Grgić is gone?" Uncle Marin thought of a solution: he would never get married but would live with his brother Nikola Grgić's family, and that way the Grgić family could stay together. He remained single and lived with my family, and my father's children were his children. He was a second father to us, and a good one, too.

In Croatia, each generation lives for the next one. Today people ask me, "Why do you keep working when you are ninety-two years old?" and I say to them, "I am not working for me, but for my daughter, my grandson, the next generation." This is the Croatian way.

Our house in Desne was made of stone. Today it is only a ruin, destroyed by the Germans during World War II, but I remember it well. It had no electricity, no running water, no modern bathroom, yet it was our shelter and our home.

At the entrance to the kitchen were several tiny holes in the wall. This was our "clock": as the sunlight came through these holes, light and shadow would move across the room, marking the passage of time like a clock. This was only one of the ways that we lived close to Mother Nature; living with awareness of Nature helped me succeed in life.

At the center of the house was a fireplace *(ognjište)* built from red bricks. The *ognjište* was used for cooking, for baking "under the *saćura*" (a lidded metal pan set on and covered with coals), and was the only source of heat. This was the heart of our home and the center of our family — the children were even born by the *ognjište*. On winter nights, we would sit around the fireplace and someone would light an oil lamp. Then we would tell stories.

We were peasants, and our life was simple. What we had, we grew or made ourselves. We even made our own musical instruments, pipes from pieces of wood that we carved. One man in Desne even had his own accordion, which he played on Sundays, and people would dance. But for most of us, we did not have money to buy things.

The first time I ever even saw a camera was when I was around six years old and my Uncle Luka came to visit from America. He brought a fine camera and said he would take my picture. First, he said, I had to put on a coat. A coat? I didn't own a coat. But I wanted my picture taken, so I put on the coat of my brother Ante, who was three years older than me. The sleeves hung over my hands, but Uncle Luka took a picture, the first one of my life, and the only one I have today from my boyhood in Desne.

Although we did not have money, we took care of ourselves. My father raised sheep and grew vegetables, wheat and lots of corn. We had fig and almond trees, and a mulberry tree, too. We would climb like monkeys to eat the fruit from that mulberry tree. We fished in the lake near our house.

Everyone worked. My Mama got up before sunrise every day. She never had a watch, but she always knew what time it was because Mother Nature never let her down. First she

All dressed up for my first picture, 6 years old.

would go to the cistern to fetch water, and then she would cut wood for cooking and for warming the house.

My Mama baked fresh bread for the family every day. I would watch her skirt swirl as she worked the stone to grind the wheat, and sometimes I would try to catch her skirt. When she finished making the dough for the bread and before putting it into the *saćura,* she would set aside a handful especially for me. She would put the small piece of dough outside on top of the hot *saćura* so it would be baked first. I waited until it was ready because it was a special treat for me — especially made for the baby. It tasted so good, better than the rest of the bread, because it was baked just for me. Instead of giving me candy, Mama would bake this small piece of bread just for me.

Maybe I was special to my parents because I was the youngest, the eleventh and last child. Sometimes Papa would cook an egg for me on the charcoals in the fireplace and he would show me how to peel it. Holding me on his knee, he would take a small piece of bread, dip it in the egg yolk and feed me like a baby bird. It was a heavenly taste!

Mama fed me with breast milk until I was two and a half years old. Then one day I misbehaved, and she said, "No more breast milk for you!" I started to cry and said, "Mama, I will die if I have no more breast milk." To this day, I remember how devastated I was because I thought I would be on breast milk forever.

But she said, "Don't worry, I will switch you from breast milk to wine." She gave me bevanda, a mixture of half water and half wine. In the middle of the table there was a large wooden *bukara* (the size of one liter) containing bevanda only for me. The rest of the family was drinking undiluted wine.

"Some day you might thank me," she said. And she was right: I liked it, and I have liked wine ever since.

Mama knew that it was safer to drink *bevanda* than water from the cistern. There was no chlorine to sterilize the rainwater that came down from the roof into the cistern, but the wine in the *bevanda* killed the harmful bugs in the water. Children would have a stomachache if they drank water from the cistern, but they would not get one if they drank *bevanda*. Or perhaps even if they had one, they would not feel the stomach pain. And *bevanda* made children happy.

I had the happiest childhood by enjoying *bevanda*. I definitely had more energy to play every day, even more than other children — I could outplay all of them!

You could say my first job was helping to make wine. At harvest, when Mama went out to help pick the grapes she would put me in a tall, wooden tank to keep me safe. She put lots of grapes into this tank. Whenever I was hungry, I could eat grapes; when I was thirsty, I could stomp the grapes and drink the juice. By the time I was three, I was helping stomp the grapes to make our wine.

Papa sold half of the wine he made and kept the rest to drink during the year. He kept the best half and sold the rest. I was surprised when I came to America and learned that here people sold the best wine instead of drinking it themselves!

My Mama wanted me to have an education so she sent

me to the village school in Desne when I was five years old, although usually children started school at six. She put a slate in her *rubac* (scarf), tied the ends, and sent me to school with my older brother Ante. This was not a success. I cried and cried so much that first day that the teacher said, "You had better go home and come back when you are six."

So I went home and became a shepherd. My Mama handed me the twenty sheep that my older brother had been taking care of. I led them up the mountain, Babina Gomila, to graze because the grass was green there. It was government land, but I didn't worry about this. It was more important to me to take the best care of my sheep and bring them home when I saw that they were plump. I was happy when they were plump because it meant that they had eaten well.

It was part of life to work. I remember one time, when I was five years old, my Mama sent me to the village of Podrujnica to help my sister Stana, who was married and had a young baby. My job was to watch the baby while she went out to take care of errands. Stana told me to stand beside the cradle and rock it. So I did, and I rocked and rocked the cradle while I was looking at the ceiling, and suddenly the cradle became lighter. I looked down and baby Filip was gone! I found him lying on the floor, awake; I had rocked him right out of the cradle. I was shocked, scared and worried that he might be hurt. I immediately picked him up, and fortunately he was smiling and unharmed. I put him back in the cradle and continued rocking him and singing baby songs to him — *Cuni nuni my little baby, cuni nuni my little baby*. Filip started to sleep again, and I did not tell my sister Stana what happened. I was

Miljenko "Mike" Grgich

afraid to lose my first job at the age of five.

When I was six, I went to school again. This time I was better at it, except I had another problem: my shoes. My Mama had made shoes for me from cow skin. She made the shoes, called *opanci*, in the shape of a boat and connected each side with thin strips of lambskin. You had to put on your socks first, then *terluci* knitted out of wool, which would also be shaped like little boats and would provide a cushion for your feet. The *opanci* were not made for rainy days. One day it was raining heavily as I walked to school. When I walked into the classroom my shoes announced my arrival. Every step produced a sound, "tsik, tsik, tsik." The students started laughing as I passed by them. The teacher called me to come show her what the noise was about. I told her my *terluci* and my shoes were wet from the rain. She said, "If your father cannot buy you good shoes, you should not come to school," but that did not stop me from going to school. I came back again the next day with the same *opanci* and everybody got used to the sound as I walked by.

Even if we were too poor to buy real shoes, our life was good. When you live close to nature like we did, making wine, growing your food, and taking care of your garden and animals, you learn things that you would not learn in school. We all knew about rain and wind and snow and sun, and about working and trading with people. You have a strong connection with others and most of all with Mother Nature.

In Desne, school ended after fourth grade. Like most Croatians, we were Catholic, and my mother wanted me to

ZAGREB **SPLIT** **DESNE** **METKOVIC**

become a priest, who would travel to other countries to make converts. There was a problem, however: you needed to have money for the first two years of study to become a priest, and we had no money for this.

So Mama had another idea: I could go live with my sister Stana, whose son I had rocked right out of his cradle, and who now lived in the larger town of Metković. There I could go to school until I was fourteen.

Even if she could not read or write, it was always important for Mama that I get an education. She was the daughter of a village doctor. Medical doctors could be found only in big cities, but the village doctors knew many remedies, and they were the ones you went to for most problems. I believe I got from her family my love of learning and the ability to absorb whatever knowledge was offered to me, although I never wanted to be a doctor myself. I liked science but not blood!

My Papa was sad to see me leave home when I was so young, only ten years old. He had tears rolling down his face as he said good-bye to me. "Son, I have no money to give you but I have advice," he said. "Try to always be with people who are smarter than you and learn from them. What you do every day, do your best. Make at least one friend every day. After one year, you will have three hundred and sixty-five friends, a value no money can buy. Remember, if you have a friend in every village, you will always have somewhere to sleep."

I took his words with me when I left home, and I have kept them with me all of my life.

The Grgić family homes today

The tiny town of Desne near the foot of Babina Gomila, with lake Modro Oko ("the blue eye").

Chapter 2

A Young Student

Perhaps it was because I grew up in a village surrounded by mountains that my idea has always been to keep moving ahead and up — never down. For me, the way to do this has been to keep learning. It has been my experience that if you have a goal, the whole world will help you achieve it. When at age 10 I wanted more education, my family helped me, as much as they could.

I went to live with my sister Ljubica and my cousin Srećko Grgić in the village Krvavac, which was about five miles from Desne on the Neretva River. From Krvavac I would go five miles on foot to a school in Metković, the Građanska Škola. Ljubica was not married, but she worked for our cousin Srećko. Srećko's father, Ivan Grgić, had gone to America and returned with enough money to open a grocery store in Krvavac. Srećko was now running the store, and when I went to live with Ljubica and him in the apartment above the store, I, too, began helping out.

Srećko became a great influence in my life. He was a good businessman; educated, hard working and intellectual. He was always reading books. When I was not in school, Srećko would teach me about running a business in his grocery store. From him I received my first lessons in managing a business.

When winter came, that walk to and from school in Metković became a long and problematic one, especially during rainy days. One day when I was returning from school to Krvavac, I was carrying a box that held all of my art papers. In one hand I had my umbrella and in the other I held the box. It was raining, and the strong wind turned my umbrella inside out. While I was trying to save the umbrella, I accidentally let go of the box. I had forgotten to tie a string around it, so the lid came off, and the papers flew off in the wind! I could see all of my artwork scattered everywhere, covering the wheat fields. I tried to collect some of the papers, but they were all so wet and muddy I gave up.

I was all wet and muddy, too, when I arrived at home. This was a problem because I had only one pair of trousers and one shirt, which I would wash at night. My sister offered me cousin Srećko's clothes to wear while my clothes were being washed and dried, and she put his heavy long coat over me so I could stay warm.

When Srećko discovered that I'd returned without the papers, he became angry that I was so careless. I explained what had happened but he said I should have picked up the muddy papers and brought them home to see if they could be salvaged. He was so angry that Ljubica got upset too, and she

Metković, where I attended school from age 10-14. You can see in the background on the right the Church of St. Ilija, which was close to where I lived.

thought she should do something to keep him from becoming angrier, so she picked up a big stick and began hitting me. Fortunately for me, her heart wasn't really in it, and Srećko's coat was long and thick. That heavy coat saved me from being bruised!

As a result of this catastrophe, it was decided that during the rainy season I should live with my sister Stana, who was now living in Metković, close to my school.

Metković, with a population of five thousand people, was a much larger town than Desne. And this continued: in the 2011 census Metković had fifteen thousand people, and Desne only one hundred and thirty.

Stana's husband, Mate Brljević, worked for the Metković post office as a telephone line supervisor. Their house was in the center of town, close to St. Ilija Catholic Church. The kitchen was downstairs, and upstairs were the bedrooms. In the front of the house was a cistern to catch the rain from the roof so they would have their own water. Years later they built an additional room near the cistern.

Stana and Mate had two sons, Filip and Ivo, and a daughter, Fila, nicknamed "Seka." Living with them, just as with my sister Ljubica, I did not feel like I had left my home altogether. I helped out whenever I could. In the mornings I would go outside and cut wood for the stove. I would go to the bakery to buy fresh hot bread to prepare breakfast for my sister and her husband so it would be ready by the time they got up, but on the way home I could smell the aroma of the freshly baked bread and could not resist breaking off the end of the loaf, called the *cica*. It tasted so good I would bring home bread without its ends!

I studied at the Građanska Škola from the age of ten to fourteen. The school was considered a comprehensive business school, so in addition to subjects like French, art and penmanship, I studied bookkeeping. During the summer I continued to work with Srećko in his grocery store. I was getting ready to be a businessman myself.

It was a busy time, and my biggest challenge was learning to be responsible for myself at such a young age. Sometimes these can be hard lessons. I remember the air of anticipation caused by the news that Bishop Quirinus Clement Bonefačić, the Bishop of the Diocese of Split-Makarska, was coming to the village of Kula Norinska, also on the Neretva River. There was great excitement because no bishop had ever been to Kula Norinska before. Bishop Bonefačić was coming for a special occasion: the people of Kula Norinska were placing a Christian cross on a fortress called Kula, which had been built centuries earlier by Moslems. One of my uncles, Don Rade Jerković, a priest, arranged for me to be an altar boy to serve at the Mass. This was quite an honor.

As always, when I went anywhere, I walked. It was a warm summer day when I set out for Kula Norinska, a mile away from Krvavac. As I walked along the Neretva River, the day got hotter and hotter. It was so hot that I stopped to wash my hands, but when I felt the cool water of the river, I could not resist taking a dip. I decided to take a quick break. To preserve my good clothes, I took them off and hung them on a tree.

I jumped into the river and it felt great to be so cool, but when I got out, I discovered that my shirt was gone! I looked everywhere, but I couldn't find it. Someone passing by must have seen it and taken it. I suppose I was lucky because they had not taken my pants too! As I went on to Kula Norinska, I asked myself, "How can I go up to the bishop without a shirt?"

When I arrived in Kula Norinska there were thousands of people gathered for the event. Without my shirt on, I stood out in the crowd, and many people turned to stare at me. I heard someone say, "Well, he looks very comfortable." Everyone, of course, had dressed up in their finest clothes for this important event. When I finally found my uncle, Don Jerković, I apologized and asked for his forgiveness because I came without my shirt. He allowed me to stay for the Mass, but I was very sorry to have missed my one opportunity to be an altar boy for the Bishop of the Diocese of Split-Makarska.

In spite of these occasional mishaps, when I finished my studies in Metković my cousin Srećko proposed an idea: he wanted to open a grocery store in Desne, and he wanted me to be the manager. I am not so sure I would trust anyone who is only fourteen years old to manage a store on his own, but Srećko thought I could do it.

When I graduated from Građanska Škola, something happened that I had never expected: my father bought me new clothes — a pair of pants, a shirt and my first pair of store-bought shoes. I have to say, I really needed those new pants. When I started school in Metković, my one pair of pants had originally come down to my ankles, protecting my legs from

PHOTOGRAPH OF KULA NORINSKA (IN THE BACKGROUND WITH THE CROSS) AND THE HIGHLY ANTICIPATED VISIT FROM THE BISHOP, WHICH I ATTENDED SHIRTLESS.

the cold in the winter and the sun during the summer. In four years, my pants had faded and acquired many patches, and they had also become shorts! My new rubber shoes, the *Bata* brand made in Czechoslovakia, were the cheapest shoes my father could find in the market but I was proud to put them on. In my new clothes I felt like a king, and my classmates were happy for me too.

When I look back, I realize how much people helped each other. I was lucky that I had so many members of the Grgić family during those years. They may not have had money, but they did what they could to help me go to school.

Many years later, I would be able to give back to my sisters by sponsoring our relatives to come to the United States. Stana's grandson Matko Brljević was able to come to the United States with my guarantee. Matko and his wife Tihana now own a pharmacy in Los Angeles. When my sister Neda's grandson, Ivo Jeramaz, wanted to come to America, I also gave him a guarantee. He lived with me for three years and I gave him a job at Grgich Hills Cellar.

When my cousin Srećko asked me to be the manager of his grocery store in Desne I thought my future had been set. I never imagined that one day I would be in a position to help my relatives come to America.

My sister Ljubica and my cousin Srećko, with whom I was living when war broke out.

Too close to home: it is a good thing we weren't living here when this bomb hit.

Chapter 3

War

*H*ow can I describe what happens when war comes to a peaceful little village like Desne?

Adolf Hitler had been on the move since he had become chancellor of Germany in 1936, but in a remote village like Desne, this had little impact on our lives. When he invaded Poland in 1939, however, and England declared war, all of Europe was affected, including my village.

I had been managing my general merchandise store for three years when the war arrived. The store was open seven days a week, and I sold everything the villagers needed, from wine to fabrics. My father brought some of his wine to the shop, and when there were bocce tournaments in town players would order liters of wine.

I lived in the rustic loft above the shop where the supplies were stored. Sometimes fishermen would wake me up in the middle of the night to buy carbide to power their lamps for night fishing. One night, after a long day of work, I was sleeping in my wooden bed covered with a *komarnjak* over me to protect me from mosquitoes, when something unexpected woke me up. It was not a fisherman wanting to buy a pound of carbide but a mouse nibbling on my ear! The *komarnjak* protected me against the mosquitoes but not from the mouse. Since my bed was on the same floor where the food supplies were stored, the mice happily thrived there, but this time they wanted to taste my ear for a change.

I worked with Srećko to keep the store supplied with other goods that came from Metković. He continued to be my business teacher, but I also found other role models. In little Desne, a neighbor had loaned me a book that filled my mind with wonder. It told the stories of American businessmen Henry Ford, Andrew Carnegie and John Rockefeller. I was fascinated to learn that they had all started life as poor men, but had worked their way up and become so successful that they were among the wealthiest men in the world. I asked myself, "Was that really possible?" Perhaps, but only in a place such as America.

Meanwhile, I was busy every day. I was learning things like how to collect money from people who hadn't paid their bills, and how to describe fabric to ladies. I had to be sure not to tell them if someone else had bought the same material — they didn't like that! My father had taught me that no matter what situation you are in, you should learn all you can to succeed. You never know when it will come in handy. And I loved learning. But I didn't realize that I was learning practical business skills that would help me when I opened my winery in America. I did not dream so big in those days.

I was back in Desne living near my parents, and that made me happy. My father was growing older and we had learned that he had lung cancer, so I was glad to be near him and to help my mother when I could.

As a working man, although still a teenager, I also took part in village life. On Sundays, after Mass at St. George's church, villagers gathered for a dance. It was the tradition, however, that a man should not ask a woman to dance if she was taller than he was. I was such a short guy and most of the women were taller than me, so even if I wanted to I could not ask them to dance. I just tapped my feet in my seat and watched everyone else enjoy dancing.

Everything changed when the war arrived.

We lived without newspapers, radios or television, so we had no contact with the greater world. Eventually the news that we were at war made its way to Desne, and with it came Italian soldiers.

In April 1941, after the Axis powers of Germany and Italy invaded and occupied Yugoslavia, they created a puppet state called the Independent State of Croatia (Nezavisna Država Hrvatska or NDH, as it was often called), comprised of most of central and northern Croatia.

Dalmatia, however, in the south, was annexed by Italy. The towns that made up my world, Desne, Krvavac and Metković, were all part of this region. It was officially proclaimed a monarchy, and Prince Aimone of Savoy-Aosta, Duke of Aosta, was appointed ruler. He refused to accept the kingship, however, because he opposed the Italian annexation of Dalmatia, where the people were Croatian, not Italian. Eventually he was pressured to accept it by King Victor Emmanuel III of Italy, but he never moved from Italy to live in Croatia. He was referred to as Tomislav II, King of Croatia.

It was said by some that the Germans wanted the Italians to occupy Dalmatia so that German soldiers could concentrate on the invasion of Russia. My own belief is that the Italians had no desire to fight in Russia when Hitler invaded that country in 1941. Instead, the Italian soldiers wanted to stay in sunny and beautiful Dalmatia where it was comfortable, rather than face the freezing winter and fierce fighting in Russia.

The Italians had a campaign to persuade the Germans that they were needed in Dalmatia, in villages like Desne, because of the threats from Communist guerilla fighters, or partisans, living in the mountains. And that meant tragedy for us when the Italian soldiers moved in and occupied our village.

One of the first things the soldiers did was to murder our priest from St. George's Church. What was his crime? He was ringing the church bell that summoned villagers to Mass. The soldiers mistakenly concluded that he was sending a signal to the partisans that the Italian soldiers were coming. The Italian soldiers dragged the priest out of bed, barefoot, told him to kneel, and shot him dead.

As word reached me in my shop that the Italian soldiers had killed our priest, I also learned that they were rounding up the men of Desne, about fifty in all, including my father. At this time he was ill in bed but this didn't stop the Italians from taking him from the house as a dangerous partisan.

When I heard this I ran out from my store to find the commander. I pleaded with him, "Please, will you let my father go home? He is old, he is dying of cancer, and he is not a danger to you."

The commander looked at me and replied, "OK, he can go home, but we will take you instead."

They took us to the cemetery by St. George's Church. Why were we in a graveyard? We believed it was the end for us, but they didn't shoot us. A message came in for the leader, and then the soldiers tied our hands. With one long rope, the soldiers bound us together and ordered us to begin marching to Kula Norinska.

We marched in silence for five miles until we came to the sandy riverbank. The soldiers ordered us to line up. In front of us was a long, deep pit they had dug in the sand. They stood behind us with their machine guns pointed at our backs. I looked up at the sky, and out at the peaceful river, and then at the grave in front of me, and the thought came to my mind, "I am going to die, but how will I know when I am dead?"

I do not know how long we stood there in the sun between the soldiers and the grave they had dug for us. What can you do? You can pray and then perhaps you will have relief. That is a good reason to have religion and have faith in God.

But then an extraordinary thing happened. I saw a *trupica* (small Neretvan boat) coming down the river, and paddling it was my sister Ljubica. As she came nearer she yelled out,

"Don't be afraid, they won't kill you. They will take you to Metković."

She had heard this in the village and she had come the fastest way she could to tell us. She was a woman of great courage.

It was true! Soon trucks pulled up and we were herded into them. They drove us to a prison in Metković, where we were taken into a room guarded by soldiers. I remember how one guard pushed his gun in my back. I started to argue, "This is my country." He hit me with the butt of his gun. To this day, I still feel sore in in the place where he hit me.

We were made to lie flat on the wooden floors. If you moved, the soldiers thought you were trying to escape, so they would point their guns at you. One by one, we were interrogated, and after four days we were released because none of us had any connection with the partisans. The only one who was not released was Mate Šetka, the husband of my sister Neda. We never saw him again. This is how war is: things happen and you don't know why, people disappear and you don't know where they have gone. Nothing makes sense.

Later we learned that Mate Šetka had been taken to a prison near Belgrade; he died there when it was bombed by the Allies. Neda was left a widow with two small children, Jelica and Ivo. I was not married, so I helped Neda and her children whenever I could. We all had to help each other in order to survive. You never knew what would happen next.

Since my father was old and sick and I was the only son left at home, I did not have to enlist in the army, but every

Kula Norinska and trupica, a traditional Croatian boat. My sister Ljubica paddled a vessel just like this to save me from an early grave.

man was given a pass and each month we were required to report to the Italian police station in Metković to have it stamped. Usually it was just a bureaucratic exercise but one month when I reported in, the officer examined my pass and, without an explanation, I was taken to the prison and locked up. All through that night, I could only wonder, what had I done? What was going to happen to me now?

It turned out that there was a well-known partisan living in the mountains, who not only had the same name as me, Miljenko Grgić, but his mother had the same name as my mother, Iva. To make matters worse, I was carrying with me my little Austrian knife that my father had given me. It was stamped with a hammer and sickle, the logo of a factory that existed in the old Austro-Hungarian Empire. When the Italians saw the knife and my name, they thought they had captured a Communist.

When I did not come home that day, my sister Ljubica walked to the police station to ask where I was. She found out that I had been taken to prison but she did not learn why. And so she did the only thing she could think of doing: she started to pray.

The next morning, the Italians discovered their mistake and admitted that I was a simple shopkeeper, not a notorious Communist. They told me I could leave. When I walked out of the prison the first person I saw was my sister Ljubica, sitting on a stone wall. She had stayed there all night praying for my safety. I could only conclude that God had heard her prayers. There have been many times in my life when I felt God was close to me, and this was one of them.

On September 8, 1943, the Italians surrendered. The Italian soldiers moved out of Dalmatia. They had left Metković but worse things were in store for us. Because then the Nazis took over Dalmatia.

I had kept the store open and running throughout the Italian occupation. I received allotments of goods and I sold them. We did not hear much news from the outside world; we didn't know who was winning but we knew that the Germans came to Desne occasionally.

Our goal was to survive but sometimes to do this you have to fight. For me the test came in an unexpected way. Near Desne there was a small village, Vrdesne, where there lived a big man, Josip Gnjeć, who was the village bully. While the Italians had occupied Metković, he had been friendly with them, and when the Germans arrived he clearly meant to be on good terms with them too.

One of the first things the Germans did was to go on a looting spree in my cousin Srećko's store in Krvavac. They were carrying off all the food to have a feast, and who was with them but the bully, Josip Gnjeć?

When Srećko rushed to the store to try to protect it, I went with him. Josip Gnjeć saw Srećko coming; he grabbed him and began to beat him. I was horrified. What could I do? I was a little guy and not used to fighting, but I had to help my cousin. The bully was hitting him again and again, and Srećko could not get free of him. I didn't know what to do so I looked around and found a stick. I thought that if I hit him on the shoulder, he might release Srećko. I swung the stick with all of my strength. Instead of hitting his shoulder, I missed and hit the side of his head, and I hit it so hard that I knocked his ear right off! He was shocked, to say the least, and so was I. It did stop the fight.

Afterwards, a surprising thing happened. The people from Vrdesne began coming to my shop in Desne bringing me gifts — a basket of eggs, a chicken — all because I had accidentally knocked the ear off the bully, Josip Gnjeć.

The Italians had been promoting the idea that Desne was a center for dangerous partisans who were living in the mountains around the village so that they would not be sent to fight on the Russian front. Evidently, they made their case too well. When the Germans arrived, they decided they would take care of this problem, and so they burned Desne to the ground.

The villagers of Desne fled, going to wherever they could find a place to stay. Like most of the others, Mama, Papa and I went where we had relatives. We went to Metković, to the house of my sister Stana.

We didn't know that by then Germany was losing the war. We only wanted to escape from the soldiers who were so brutal and destructive and held such power over our lives.

By then I was twenty years old. My brother Ante had been drafted to fight in the Croatian army, but I had not, because whenever I saw German soldiers, I would hide. One time as I saw them coming down a street in Metković, I ran into an unfinished house that was next to my sister's home. There was a boat on the ground floor. I jumped inside it and pulled

Axis occupation of Yugoslavia 1941–43

the canvas cover over me. It was only later that I realized I had only covered half of myself — my head was under the cover, but my backside was not! Fortunately, the soldiers didn't come into the house and so they missed me. Another time I scrambled to the upper floor of the unfinished house, but this time the soldiers came into the house. Because the floor was not complete, I could see them below me. They stopped to light their cigarettes and lit a fire in the fireplace. The smoke drifted up to where I was hiding. All I could think was, "Dear God, please, don't let me sneeze." Thankfully, I didn't sneeze, and they left without seeing me. (It was another miracle!)

I have kept my parents' memory, their spirit, and their wisdom with me all of my life. Not long after we came to Metković, my Papa died of lung cancer. When the war ended in 1945 and the German occupiers left, my Mama returned to Desne, where she passed away in 1946 from the stomach ailments that had always plagued her. At the time I was sick and hospitalized in Dubrovnik. My sister Ljubica came to Dubrovnik to tell me, but even before she arrived I knew from a dream that our Mama had died. Ljubica and I held each other's hands and cried.

Desne, which had been such a happy and prosperous place for centuries, was in ruins like so many other places in Europe. Only a stone shell was left of the house where I was born and lived as a boy.

For people who have never lived through a war that comes uninvited, destroys your home and murders your family and friends, it is probably hard to understand what it is like. You have no power when foreign soldiers take over your village. You never know what their next move will be. But I learned that this ignites in people the will to survive. You know that if you can live through this, you can endure anything. This was a good thing to learn because it gave us the courage to face what was in store for Croatia next — Communism.

Josip Broz Tito rode into power in 1945 and held the reins for decades, establishing first a communist and then a socialist state.

Chapter 4

The Communists Take Power

No one can truly describe those weeks we endured as the war ended. As with all wars, it was the common people who suffered, and when the war ended, their misery did not. In Croatia, still part of Yugoslavia, the year 1945 was one of complete confusion for most people. Things were out of control. No one knew what would happen.

During the war, the leader of the Communist partisans fighting in the mountains of Yugoslavia was Josip Broz Tito, who had been born in Croatia and had spent ten years in Russia, where he prepared himself to organize Communism in Yugoslavia.

We knew of the Communist partisans. They were lawless people: from time to time, they came into the village to ask for food, clothing and supplies. They would send letters to my store asking me to provide them with food or they would come and take it. Here was a problem: if you did not help them, the partisans might kill you, and if you helped them, you would likely be killed by the German occupiers or by the Independent state of Croatian, the NDH. We had already seen both German soldiers and the Communists kill several villagers. When the partisans finally came looking for me to loot my store, a friend had fortunately already warned me, and I had escaped in the middle of the night, first hiding in my friend's basement and then swimming across the lake to Komin. They cleaned out everything from the store, but I had saved my life. I was now on the list of people to be killed, and it was always a question of how to survive when there was danger on all sides.

As the war ended, it seemed to me that the powers in the West didn't really care what happened in a remote country like Yugoslavia. I read a report that Winston Churchill's son, Randolph, was in Yugoslavia during the war. Churchill had sent him to Croatia to investigate: he wanted to know the facts about what was going on there. On one hand he was getting news that all the rebels in the mountains were partisans (Communists). From the other side he was being told that all partisans were Serbs, from the army of the Serbian King Peter. They were the King's partisans but not Communists.

When Randolph returned home he told his father, "They are all Communists there."

Churchill replied, "Yes, Communists took over, but don't worry, son, you are not going to live there."

The Soviet Union moved in as the Germans left Yugoslavia at the end of the war. Tito, the partisan, was installed as the new leader of Yugoslavia.

The transition was terrible for the people. Communism brought chaos. There were no established laws. You did not know what to expect or who was in charge. You were never sure that you would be alive tomorrow. Some people got out while they could; they went to Australia, Italy or America. America was a magnet for people from all over the world. Italy was nearby, and it was even easier to go to Australia than America, but most of the people who wanted to get out from under Communism wanted to go to America because they had relatives there.

The coming of Communism created a life that normal Americans can't imagine. If you owned a business, they would take everything you owned and then kill you. When the Communists came to Desne, they looted everything from my store. Luckily, I was warned that they were looking for me, that I was on their "to-be-killed list." I escaped to Metković and survived the first blow of the post-war world.

Communism was devastating for people who were intelligent and educated — they were considered the enemy. People were there one day, and gone the next.

Before the war, I read what I could to learn about Communism in Russia. They preached that they would take over, country by country, and soon the whole world would be Communist. Most people believed it was true, and that the Communists would never leave our country now that they had come in.

Some joined the Communist party: it was the way to get ahead. But I could not. I knew I couldn't be a member of this party. I didn't fit in with their ideas. There was no individualism.

When the Communists took over in Yugoslavia, they tried to control everything. Even farmers had to wait for permission from Belgrade, the capital of Yugoslavia, to plant their crops. One time when I was sick and needed to see a doctor, I had to wait so long for an appointment that a friend of mine suggested that I go lie down in the street and pretend that I had been hit by a car. "Then maybe you will be seen by a doctor," he said. My friend may have been joking, but I actually tried this. But all that happened was that the police thought I was drunk and brought me to the hospital, where I was put in a room with the drunkards.

Another thing that I realized was that I wanted to keep my religion. I had been raised Catholic. The Communists wanted us to forget that and believe only in them. I couldn't do this. Our religion had been an important part of our life in Desne. I believed in God, not Communists. The Communist notion of equality was a joke. Some people lived lives of great privilege, but for the common people nothing got better. They could only just try to stay alive.

One strategy that helped people survive was telling stories, many making fun of the government. A popular tale went like this: In Belgrade, a street sweeper was at work. He would sweep and then pause and hold his broom vertically to observe the shadow it made. The Russian soldiers on duty watched this man in amazement until one soldier marched over to the sweeper. "Why do you put the broom vertical?" he demanded.

The sweeper replied, "By the shadow of the broom, I know when it is time for lunch."

The soldier grabbed the sweeper's broom. "Give me the watch!" he shouted.

Another story told of a man who was walking with a pack on his back. A thief jumped on him and took the pack. He opened it and discovered it was full of Yugoslavian money. He emptied it, took the backpack and left the money; the pack was worth more than the money!

Amidst all of this chaos, I had to think of what my own future would be. Communism had destroyed my dreams. I could not possibly have a store. How could I salvage my life? What would be my future?

A Croatian folktale I have taken to heart because it is applicable to every situation is about an oak tree and a willow. The oak would brag to the willow how strong he was and how weak the poor willow was, bending at every gust. When a violent storm came and a stong wind was blowing, the oak tree broke and fell into the creek. The oak tree looked up at the willow, which was still upright by the creek, and said, "How can I, a mighty oak, be felled while you are still standing in the same place?"

The willow replied, "You are so big and strong that you do not bend when a strong wind blows. I, a willow, am flexible and pliant. When a strong wind blows, I bend; when the wind stops I can straighten up."

Living under Communism, it was necessary to bend like the willow so that you could survive and be alive tomorrow.

Miljenko "Mike" Grgich

For me, education was always the means to move onward and upward. I decided that somehow I would go back to school. But what would I study?

There was a need for bookkeepers, and with my business background, I decided that this would be the perfect job for me. About 153 kilometers north of Metković was the city of Split where there was a business college with a three-year program that would qualify a person to become an accountant.

I went to Split. Education was free, but I didn't have the money to live in Split as a full-time student, and so I got the idea that I could be a "private" student. I bought the books for the classes and took them back to Metković where I studied them at home. A month before the term ended, I went back to Split and sat in the classes as the teachers reviewed everything they had covered during the academic year. I would then take the final exams with the students. I passed the tests each year, and after three years, I received my degree in business. When you really want to do something, there is a way to accomplish it, even when the Communists are in charge.

With my hard-earned degree in hand, I returned to Metković, where I found work as an accountant for the town's Co-op. I worked there for one year, and at the end of this year, I looked at what I had achieved. I had filled two cabinets with papers. I thought, "If I work for thirty-five years, what would have I accomplished then? I would have 70 cabinets filled with papers."

Was this the life I wanted? No. I concluded it was not

DESPITE MY CIRCUMSTANCES I ALWAYS HAD HOPE, AND A BELIEF IN EDUCATION.

for me. But what life did I want? I searched my soul to find my answer, and I decided I would return to the work that my father had done. I would carry on my family's tradition. I would go back to the instincts that had guided all the generations before me. I would make wine.

Zagreb, a university city since 1669.

Chapter 5

To Zagreb

I did not know what destiny had in store for me when I decided to become a winemaker. Wine was my heritage, but this was also a practical decision. I realized that wine was something I could always sell. People like to celebrate with wine in good times, but it also helps them forget in bad times. In fact, it adds pleasure to any day. During the war, we had to pull out some of my father's grapevines to plant vegetables so that we would not go hungry. In retrospect I have wondered if maybe we should have kept the vines and made wine to sell for money to buy vegetables on the black market.

My Papa had taught me the art of winemaking, but when I decided to make it my profession, I knew it was time to learn the science and technology of winemaking because great wine is the result of both art and science. To learn the science, however, meant taking a step that no one in my family had ever taken before: I would need to go to the university in the faraway city of Zagreb.

ॐ Miljenko "Mike" Grgich

Zagreb is the largest city in Croatia, and today it is the capital of the independent country of Croatia. The University of Zagreb is the largest and oldest university in Southern Europe. At that time, it had a department of enology and viticulture but only twelve new students were admitted each year. I was determined to be one of those students.

I set out for Zagreb, the furthest I had ever been from my home. Zagreb, in the north, is inland from the sea. It is about five hundred kilometers, or three hundred miles, from Desne.

When I arrived in the city I wanted to be first in line when the university opened the enrollments for the spots in the enology and viticulture program. It was about three miles from my rented room to the University of Zagreb. The streetcars didn't start running until 5:30 a.m., so my friend Ivo Đerek and I got up at 2 a.m. and started walking to the university. When we arrived, a young lady was already in line! We camped out on the ground in front of the office but no one else showed up until the streetcars started running. When the office opened, I got my place.

I had only a little savings from my work as an accountant, but I was able to enroll in the university because education was free, which was the only good thing about Communism. There was no tuition to pay, but then I had to figure out how I was going to live as a full-time student in a city far from my family and friends. My father and mother had passed away; I had no one to help me, and there were no such things as student loans. I don't think I would have chosen to borrow money anyway; it is not the Croatian way to be in debt.

I AM THE SECOND ONE FROM THE RIGHT,
WITH MY FRIEND IVO ĐEREK, THIRD FROM THE RIGHT,
AT THE INSTITUTE FOR POMOLOGY.

∽ Miljenko "Mike" Grgich

I found a room in a mansion that was more than one hundred years old and had been converted into housing. My room was in the servants' quarters, and the bed must have been just as old as the house. The mattress had a big hole in the middle which was covered with a sheet of aluminum. When you tried to sleep, you fell in the hole and could not turn right or left. I went home after the first term to spend time with my family and brought back my sleeping mat from Metković, so at least I had a mattress.

This was all I had in that room. I didn't have heat or running water or even a table. In the winter it was too cold and the light was too poor to study in this room. To keep warm I would go to a café or hotel between lunch and dinner services and order a glass of water. I would sip it slowly as I studied all afternoon. When the dinner guests began to arrive, I would leave and go back to my cold room.

Many people have asked me, "Why do you wear a French beret?" Well, one rainy day when I got off of a streetcar, I happened to leave my umbrella behind. By the time I noticed I had lost it, the streetcar and my umbrella were both gone. I was so poor that I did not have enough money to buy another umbrella, so I told myself, "All I need is something to protect my head when it rains."

I walked the streets of Zagreb and saw different hats in the display windows until a French beret caught my eye. I told myself, "That beret is very practical. It will protect my head from the rain, and when I'm not wearing it I can fold it up and keep it in my pocket so I won't lose it."

I never could have guessed that one day this same beret would be in the great Smithsonian Institution in Washington, D.C., the capital of the United States of America. Who could have imagined this? As I look back now, I know that world events formed my life, but it also seems to me that something else exists that is just as important. You may plan and set goals, and this is good, but your life is led not only by your own desires but by something else, by destiny, together with God and the influence of family and friends.

Those years in Zagreb as a poor student were hard, but I was learning. In all, I studied more than forty subjects, including chemistry and botany. I supported myself by working two research jobs. One was in the Genetics Institute of the University working on creating new forms of wheat. We had a problem growing wheat in Croatia because it grew tall, and the winds and rain would beat it down and break it. Rye, on the other hand, was short and sturdy. My job was to see if we could crossbreed the two and create a new kind of wheat that would not fall down when it rained. In my second job at the Institute of Pomology, I did research to create new varieties of fruit.

My last two years in the university were mostly dedicated to studying enology (winemaking) and viticulture (grape growing). I began work on my thesis, which was a study of the varieties of grapes growing in Neretva River Valley in Metković. In this area alone I found more than fifty varieties of grapes. When I thought about it, however, it made sense. For centuries Croatia had been a crossroads of influences; Greeks, Romans, Hungarians and Italians had all passed through the country, and no doubt they had planted grapevines.

I was learning outside of the university as well. I remembered the stories I had read about successful people in the United States of America, such as Henry Ford, Andrew Carnegie and the Rockefellers. It seemed to me that if a person put his mind to it, he could achieve far more than he expected; even those men had not dreamed of what they would achieve. But they had an advantage: they were in America.

The idea of America as a world of opportunity was not what the Communists portrayed to us in the news. Nothing they reported about America was ever good. We were told it was a country full of crime and violence, of great inequality and poverty for most of the people. They would show pictures of rats running through hospitals to prove how bad life was there. What was the truth, I wondered. Then, I got an answer that changed my life.

By 1954 the Communist grip on life in Yugoslavia was beginning to ease up a little. People were allowed to travel out of the country again, and one of my professors, Professor Šerman, from the Department of Viticulture and Enology, went to California on sabbatical leave for six months. When he returned, we were bursting with questions and wanted to know what it was like in the United States. But Professor Šerman avoided us; it was clear that he was afraid to talk to us for fear the Communists would hear his opinions. Finally, one day several of us found him alone in a room, and we asked him, "Tell us: What was it like in this place, California?"

He looked around as if he were checking to see if the secret police might be listening. When he was sure it was safe, he put his hand over his mouth and whispered, "California is Paradise!"

"Where there is no water," he added, "it is a desert. But where there is water, it is Paradise."

All the way home that day his words rang in my head like a bell tolling: California-Paradise-California-Paradise. It started me thinking: Why should I wait until I die to go to Paradise? Why not walk into Paradise while I am alive?

I began to look for a way to get to this Paradise — California — and I got an idea. At that time in Yugoslavia students were being allowed to leave the country temporarily for internships through a United Nations exchange program. I had nearly completed my four years of studies at the university. I just had to finish my thesis to get my diploma. I knew, however, that once I had my university degree, I would not be permitted to leave the country. So I applied for the student exchange program, and my work in genetics was helpful to me. I was accepted for a two-month internship in Austria for the harvest of 1954. My fellow classmate, Ivo Sokolić, had been accepted to West Germany, but he really wanted to go to Austria to visit a professor he knew. All I wanted was to escape Yugoslavia, so I was happy to exchange places with him. This student exchange program gave me the opportunity to obtain two valuable things: a passport and a ticket to Germany. It was also the beginning of my lifelong friendship with Ivo Sokolić, who went on to become a well-known author of numerous books on grapes and wine.

I began collecting American dollars where I could find them. I got a few dollars from my sister Ljubica and purchased some with money from my savings. In all, I came up with thirty-two dollars — what riches! I thought. With thirty-two dollars, I was sure I could buy a piece of America, if I could only get there.

I had a big obstacle ahead of me. There were guards and inspections when crossing the border, and it would be a problem to take the money with me. If the inspectors found you were carrying foreign money, it would be confiscated and most likely they would take your passport too. Even if you didn't end up in jail, you would not be leaving the country.

While I was secretly making my plans, something happened to speed them up and to reaffirm that I wanted to leave this Communist regime.

Our favorite professor was Marko Mohaček. He was a well-educated man with a sharp mind and a lot of energy. In those days, we didn't have textbooks. The professors would just talk and you would catch as much as you could, but Marko had written books for each of his subjects: organic and inorganic chemistry, analytical chemistry, and biochemistry. He had an experimental farm where he grew different varieties of potatoes, tomatoes, and grapes. He taught us chemistry, but we went to him with other questions, too, especially about wine.

Although he didn't teach enology, he was very knowledgeable about wine. One time I brought him some wine I had made, and he tasted it. "It's good," he told me, but a few minutes later he came to find me. "There's an aftertaste in your wine," he said. "Did you put sugar in it?" I had. He could tell.

In addition to being a fine teacher and a smart man, Professor Mohaček truly loved his students, and we had great respect and affection for him. We were worried when he got in trouble with the Communists.

This is how it happened: The professors at the university were all required to take a class from the government on Communism that was taught by a general who had no more than a fourth grade education. The general used a manual about Communism that had been translated from the Russian language.

Although Professor Mohaček was planning to retire soon, he had to take the class. He bought the manual and read it carefully. He wrote down the mistakes and contradictions he found in it, and at the next class he submitted to the general thirteen pages that outlined the errors. The general did not appreciate this. This was Professor Mohaček's first mistake.

The second mistake was when the general posed the question in class, "Do you believe in God?"

Marko said, "Yes, I do."

This was not in keeping with Communist teachings that wanted the people to believe only in the state. The general asked Marko, "How can you believe in God when you can't see him?"

Marko answered, "In Croatia, believing is not seeing." This was another mark against him.

◈ Miljenko "Mike" Grgich

The class on Communism was cancelled, and not long after this, Marko came into our classroom looking crushed. The dean of the university had told him that he was going to be retired immediately. This was only two months before he would have officially retired with a full pension. Being forced to take an early retirement meant he would get only seventy-five percent of his full retirement pay after a lifetime of teaching. He was being punished.

I was one of five students who decided we would try to help our professor. We went to the dean and asked for a meeting. We explained that we were due to take our final exams in two months. Professor Mohaček was the one who had been teaching us for four years. Could he stay until we had passed our exams? The answer was "No," and he was dismissed from the university.

It didn't end here for us students, however. A few days after we had gone to the dean, a friend whispered to me, "Miljenko, I think you are being followed by the Secret Police."

Now I was terrified for my life. We all knew what could happen. One day you would see a person, and the next day he would be gone and no one ever saw him again. I knew I had to get out of Croatia as soon as I could. I had my passport and my thirty-two dollars. I had to figure out a way to get out of the country with it.

I went to a shoemaker, a man that I trusted, and I took a chance. I asked, "Do you think you could take the sole off my shoe and put my money into it, then put the sole back on?" He was a good man; he didn't ask me why, but he hid the money in the sole of my shoe. I was so careful of my shoes after that, I didn't take them off. I think I even slept in them.

I had to leave in complete secrecy. This meant I couldn't tell anyone that I was leaving. I knew my sisters and brothers would understand; they had always encouraged me to leave if I got the chance. But I couldn't tell them goodbye. I was lucky that I already had a passport and a German visa. If someone who hated me heard I was leaving the country they might stop me. I was scared all the time as I made my hurried preparations to escape.

I had gotten a little suitcase, a cheap one made of cardboard. I packed it with my most important belongings: a few clothes and fifteen textbooks about viticulture and winemaking. These, I knew, would be my way to make my fortune in Paradise.

I had to leave before graduation and without my diploma, but this didn't matter to me as much as the idea of freedom, the freedom to think, to speak, and to achieve what I could. I was thirty-one years old when I set forth in search of a better future in an unfamiliar world.

I put on my beret, took my suitcase and went to the train station. As the train pulled out of Zagreb, I knew I was leaving behind everyone I knew and loved in the world. Even after I was on the train I was still afraid that I would be stopped at the border, that the guards would find the money in my shoe and I would never be allowed to leave.

As we reached the Austrian border, the train stopped. We all had to get off and go through the border inspection. I watched the guards question one woman. They took her away, and she did not come back to the train.

Nervously I waited for my turn. They asked me questions and looked at my passport, but they didn't inspect my shoes. Although I could breathe a little better when they stamped my passport and I could get back on the train, I did not relax until we began to move again.

We crossed the border. I had left Croatia. I did not think I would ever return to my country or ever again see the people I had left behind.

I was going forward to a better life. I was alone, but I was taking with me the wisdom of many teachers, including my parents and Professor Marko Mohaček, an intelligent man who believed in God, even though he could not see Him. I believed in God, too, that He was everywhere, and He was traveling with me, on my way to a new world.

How did I feel? I felt free.

THE SUITCASE THAT I CARRIED WITH ME TO AMERICA IN ITS FIRST EXHIBIT AT THE SMITHSONIAN INSTITUTION MUSEUM OF AMERICAN HISTORY.

The Franck farm by Schwäbisch Hall, Germany, was called "Oberlimpurg".

Chapter 6

Escape

Mile after mile, I watched from my window as the train made its way west through the mountains of Austria and into the farmland of Germany. Every stop interested me — the sights of the towns and people were all so new and different for me, I forgot to worry about what my future might be. I was moving ahead as fast as the train could take me.

It was late at night when we finally arrived at my destination, the small town of Schwäbisch Hall, which lies between Frankfurt and Stuttgart in the German state of Baden-Würtenberg.

At this time Germany was divided into East and West; the West was in turn, cut into three sections administered by the Americans, the French and the British. Baden-Würtenberg was in the American sector.

It was too late to call my host family, so that night I slept on a wooden bench in the train station. This didn't bother me — I'd taken the first long step toward getting to Paradise! In the morning, an attendant who worked at the train station made the call for me to Hannfried Franck, whose farm I would be working on for the next two months. Soon Mr. Franck arrived in a pickup truck, and we drove to his farm. I saw then that Schwäbisch Hall was a beautiful town on a river, with old wooden buildings in a half-timbered style quite different from the stone houses with red tile roofs in Croatia.

I had been fortunate in my assignment. Luck or perhaps a miracle was once again on my side because the Francks treated me like one of their large family, which included three daughters and two sons. Peter, who was fifteen then, was like a younger brother to me. I had a comfortable room and we all ate meals together and prayed before each meal. I could say only a few German words at first, but after a while I picked up enough of the language to communicate.

The Franck farm was about 100 hectares, or 247 acres, not far from Limburg Castle. It was an experimental farm where Mr. Franck worked on developing new varieties of grains. They grew mostly wheat. He was successful in his work, and today the seeds he developed are sold all over the world.

I was not working in a laboratory but in the fields during harvest. I was a laborer, but everyone on the farm, including the family, worked hard. My job was to ride on the harvester, to fill the one hundred and twenty-pound sacks with grain, tie them shut and transfer them to a trailer. I didn't weigh much more than the sacks, and picking up the sacks and carrying them made my fingers stretch until they were numb.

Mr. Franck had also established a school on his farm for young people. Boys learned farming and girls learned housekeeping skills. In all, about twenty people worked on the Franck farm, so there was always a lively group of young people.

Many things were new to me, like their modern farming equipment and the motorbikes. Everyone, even the youngest working students, rode motorbikes. One day a group of students thought they would play a joke on me and told me, "Here, take a ride."

They pumped the motorbike full of gas, turned it on and gave it to me, and off I went riding across a field, jumping over bales of wheat. Suddenly I saw that I was going downhill and I got scared. I had to do something to stop the motorbike but I realized that I had not been told where the brakes were. I didn't know how to stop! The tank was full of gas so I knew it would not run out soon. I didn't know what else to do, so I decided to tip the motorbike over to the left so it would stop. The motorbike stopped but it landed right on top of my left leg. I ended up with a big wound that made it difficult for me to walk for two months. I learned the benefit and the danger of motorization, which we didn't have in Croatia.

Still, we all had good times working together, and when my two-month internship was over, I had made up my mind: I was not going to return to Yugoslavia and Communism. I'd had enough of it and I'd had a taste of what it was like to work hard for yourself, as the Francks did. I'd experienced what it was like to be free and not to live in fear of who might be following you or listening to you. I thanked the Francks and told them my plan — and went to Frankfurt to apply for political asylum.

I was in for a shock. At this time, in 1954, I was one of twelve million refugees from Eastern Europe all asking for asylum in West Germany. Even though I hoped to go on to America, millions of others had this idea too, and there was a limit on the number of people from each country that the United States would admit.

Instead of getting asylum and an identity card, I was sent to an internment camp near Nuremberg. I never will forget that experience. When people talk about refugee camps today, I get chills in my spine. In this camp I found nothing but misery; people who had no present, no future, and little hope. They were fatherless, motherless, and homeless, and I had become one of them. "This," I thought, "is the end of my quest to reach America."

I had never felt such despair. But when I was at my lowest point I found a little chapel that someone had built in the camp, and I went inside. There was a statue of the Virgin Mary and in front of it a wooden bench to kneel on. I was a grown man, thirty-one years old, but tears were rolling down my cheeks as I knelt down on the little bench. All I could do was pray, "Holy Mary, Mother of God, help me."

My prayer was answered. Back in Schwäbisch Hall, the Francks were waiting for me to return and when I did not, Mr. Franck set out in search of me. He discovered what had happened and came to the camp. Because the Francks were a respected family, he was able to get my release by guaranteeing that I could live with his family and that they had work for me.

It was a miracle, and I went from total desperation to total happiness as we drove away from the camp.

I could have been happy living with the Francks but it wasn't my goal to stay in Germany. I still dreamt of California and "Paradise." I applied to Catholic Charities in America for help and eventually received a letter signed by Francis Joseph Cardinal Spellman, the archbishop of the Archdiocese of New York. It said that everything had been arranged for me to come to America, and that in two months I would arrive there. They even sent me a new suit to wear. I waited every day for a letter to arrive with my transatlantic ticket and I became a familiar face at the post office, just checking to see if a cable had been sent, but I heard nothing else after that one letter.

Meanwhile, I was working harder than I ever had in my life, at jobs I had never imagined myself doing. When harvest was over, there was still much to do. In the coldest days of the year I went out in the fields on the manure spreader. This is the best time for this task, because the ground is frozen then and the heavy wheels of the manure spreader won't compact the soil. The people who do this work are also nearly frozen. This was hard for me because I was not used to the fierce cold of German winters and I discovered that I did not like being cold. My hands were so frozen I could barely move them, and I could see ice hanging from the end of my nose.

In the spring, we began to plant in the plots of the

∽ Miljenko "Mike" Grgich

experimental farm. The goal was to test which seeds grew the best, and these blocks were so small there was not enough room for a tractor or even a horse and plow. Instead, two of us would work together: one man would put straps over his shoulder and pull the plow while the second one pushed. My job was to pull. I knew I was the workhorse, but I didn't mind doing it because it was for the advancement of knowledge and the creation of new and better crops — it was progress.

I had my books on viticulture, and I made it my practice to learn whatever I could from the vineyards in the area. During cold nights in springtime when there was a threat of frost, I saw that the farmers would spray the vines with water. Why? I wondered. Well, it turned out that the water would freeze into ice that would encase and protect the tender new buds on the vines. I remembered this many years later when I came to Napa Valley and saw that during frosts they would burn tires and light smudge pots in the vineyards to warm up and protect the grapes, and the valley would be filled with smoke. The water idea was much better and safer but you had to have a lot of water and sprinklers were very expensive in those days. Gradually farmers got more money for grapes; some had enough water in reservoirs and little by little you could see more sprinklers and less smoke in the valley during frost. Nowadays water sprinklers and wind machines are used instead, so no more smog from smudge pots in Napa Valley.

A year went by. Letters arrived from the government in Yugoslavia telling me to come back and I threw them away. I began to see wrinkles and furrows on my face from my worries. What was my future going to be?

Internment at Nuremberg, hard labor on the farm and waiting over a year for my American visa took a toll on me.

Still, hope was in my mind, and it never left me. I read and re-read my textbooks so that I would not forget what I had learned. I told myself, "Some day I will have my own little winery in Paradise." All I needed was that visa to America. One day, a friend of mine said, "Why don't you try to go to Canada?" He said he had heard that it was much easier to get visas for Canada, and Canada was right next to America.

I remembered the story of the willow and the oak and I decided it was time again to bend. I went to the Canadian Consulate. They said, "Do you have the money to go?"

I replied that if I got a visa, I would get the money. "Well," they said, "do you want to go tomorrow?"

Another miracle.

I also learned that I could get a visa to go to Australia. Now, I had a choice: which way would I go? While I tried to make up my mind, I had a dream one night about a river. It was flowing fast with muddy water and it separated into two directions. When I woke up, I knew that whatever path I chose would take me into a different life. I felt in my dream that Canada was the closer path to my destination, California.

I went back to the Canadian Consulate. They told me that they needed lumberjacks in the Yukon. Here I was, a little guy who had studied to be a winemaker and did not like the cold, and I was going to end up being a lumberjack in the Yukon. How was that going to help me get to California? But if I could only get to Canada, even the cold Yukon, I felt that I was that much closer to America. I felt happy and relieved when my passport was finally stamped with a visa to Canada.

I would take the train to Hamburg and a ship from Hamburg to Nova Scotia, Canada. Now I had to get my tickets and I needed $150 to pay for them.

I never met my oldest sister, Manda. Before I was born she had left Desne for America. There is a romantic story about her: When she was a young woman, she was with a group of women on a small boat, a *trupica* as we called them. As they went down the River Neretva, they noticed a group of young men working with the rocks on the riverbank. In particular, she was looking at one young man, and he looked up at her too. For an instant, their eyes met, and then the women sailed on. She never thought she would see him again, yet, several years later, when she went to live in Aberdeen, Washington, who did she meet but that same handsome man. "It's you!" she said, and not long after, they were married. She was the sister who would send the family in Desne five dollars each year at Christmas.

Although by this time Manda had died, her husband, Vide Domandich, was still living. I called him and explained to him my plan. He agreed to loan me the money for my tickets. I wanted to leave as soon as possible.

Anxiously I waited and waited for the money from my brother-in-law. Each day I watched for the postman, but no letter arrived for me. I would walk to the post office to check again. Had a letter come? Every day, the answer was no. Day after day went by and the money did not come. Finally it was the day before I was supposed to leave and still there was no money.

I had lived for eighteen months with the Franck family

∾ Miljenko "Mike" Grgich

and they had treated me like their own son. Still, I was surprised and shocked when Mr. Franck advanced me the $150 for my tickets. The Francks even organized a party for me the night before my departure. The whole family attended, and so did the people who worked on the farm. Everyone was celebrating that I was going to realize my dream, but this is when it struck me: I was leaving Europe and everyone I knew. I was going again into an unknown world. During my time in Germany I had learned that you can plan your life and yet something unexpected can turn those plans upside-down. I was scared. It was Mr. Franck who reassured me that this was not the time to turn back but to go forward.

The next morning, at 7 a.m., the postman made a special trip to the Franck house. He came to deliver a letter for me. The $150 from America had arrived just in time.

I paid Mr. Franck back, and the family drove me to the station to catch my train to Hamburg. I never forgot the Francks; they had become my second family. We always remained friends and when I visited them again many years later, I brought the Franck family two cases of my wine. For my ninetieth birthday in April 2013, Peter Franck sent me a bouquet of flowers.

HANNFRIED AND GERTRUD FRANK,
WHO HELPED ME MORE THAN
WORDS CAN EXPRESS.

A Glass Full *of* Miracles

~

Youth and Early Influences

Desansko Jezero (Desne Lake) and the Neretva River delta from the ruins of my home.

The home in Desne where I was born and grew up.

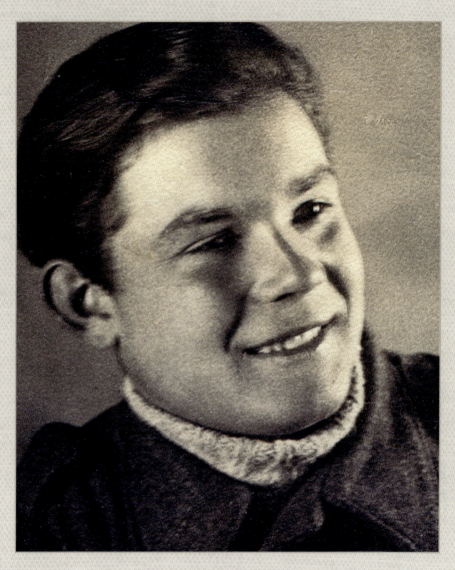

Filip Brljević fortunately survived
my babysitting adventure
and grew up into a fine young man.

Traditional opanke (moccasins), trluci (wool liners), and wood bukara (mug).

A TRADITIONAL SAĆURA COVERED WITH HOT COALS IS STILL USED FOR BAKING BREAD.

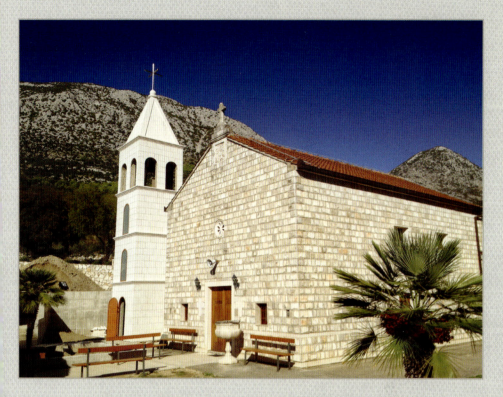

St. George church in Desne. During the war, Italian soldiers shot the priest for the crime of ringing the bell.

The cross and Plaque on Kula Norinska were placed there during the Bishop's visit when I lost my shirt.

My sister Neda, back right, with her daughter Jelica (now Jeramaz) and family. Her husband was arrested inexplicably and died in a Belgrade prison.

Ivo Đerek, with whom I studied at the University of Zagreb and a lifelong friend.

Professor Šerman, who inspired my dream to find Paradise on earth —California.

Marko Mohaček, my favorite teacher in the University. A fine professor — but he made a lousy Communist.

The wedding of my oldest sister, Manda, to her love at first sight, Vide.

My sister Manda Domandich, whom I never met, with her son Anthony before he became a priest.

A WHEAT HARVESTER AT THE FRANCK FARM, CIRCA 1950, PROBABLY THE SAME ONE I HELPED OPERATE.

Me, among Riesling grapes, during a field trip to the Rhine.

Workers and students at the Franck farm.
I am in the front row, far right.

Chapter 7

The New World

To be an immigrant takes guts. I learned this in the nine days it took to cross the Atlantic Ocean aboard the ship *Italia* from Hamburg, Germany, to Halifax, Canada.

It was winter and the passage was stormy. I am sure that eighty percent of the people on the Italia were seasick. You would see them one day but not again on the next. Still, if our crossing was rough, I think there was no comparison with the experiences of the first settlers who came to America, who did not know where they were going or how long it would take to get there. Each day, however, I had a little more hope for my future; maybe that is why I wasn't seasick.

At last we arrived in Halifax, the Canadian port city on the edge of the Atlantic Ocean. I went through customs and received my immigration papers. Did I have any relatives in Canada, I was asked. "No," I said. I got a nametag to wear on my jacket and directions to go by train to Vancouver; an immigration officer would meet me and arrange for my transportation to the Yukon, where I was going to be a lumberjack.

I did not have any friends or relatives in Canada but I did know two people in the vast new world of North America — my sister Manda's husband, Vide, and his son, Father Anthony Domandich, who was a priest in Seattle, Washington, not far from Vancouver. I used some of my precious supply of money to make a telephone call. "I am here in Halifax, Nova Scotia," I said, "and I am on my way to Vancouver and then the Yukon."

"When you get to Vancouver, check for messages at the train station's information desk," Father Anthony told me. Then I got on the train for the five-day journey that would take me 3,946 miles across the entire country of Canada.

Since my future was unknown, I did not want to spend any money if I didn't have to. I wanted to keep the $32 in my shoe for when I got to California, but life in this new world was more expensive than I had expected. On the train, when I became hungry I went into the dining car. I studied the menu and I didn't know the words. But I could read the numbers, so of course I was focusing on the right side of the menu more than on the left! When the waiter came to my table, I pointed to the cheapest thing on the menu, which was seventy-five cents.

He immediately brought me a plate with a piece of buttered toast on it. I waited to get the rest of my food before eating the toast. I watched everyone else getting their plates and enjoying their meals. Finally the waiter asked me if something was wrong. With gestures and my broken English,

A Glass Full of Miracles

I explained that I was waiting for my food. He pointed to the menu and then to the toast and said, "That's your order." That's how I understood that my seventy-five cents had bought just this one piece of buttered toast. I ate it and never returned to the dining car for the rest of the trip to Vancouver.

Instead, I got off the train at the station stops and bought bread, cheese and salami at a much cheaper price so I could stretch out my dollars until I started working. I still remember my first cultural shock when I went into a bakery in Montreal. The woman behind the counter asked what I wanted, and I knew the word for "bread." Do you have bread? I asked. She looked at me and waved her arms. "Everything you see around you is bread," she said. Bread? All I could see were plastic bags full of strange, sliced white stuff. In Europe, you bought whole wheat bread in a solid, substantial loaf and you carried the heavy loaf in your hands, sometimes even warm from the oven. You knew that it would fill your stomach. I bought a plastic bag from her but I could not call it bread.

As you can imagine, I was pretty hungry by the time the train got to Calgary in Western Canada. A woman boarded the train and sat down next to me. I immediately smelled something wonderful but, no, it was not her perfume. She was carrying a basket and when she opened it I saw it contained a barbecued chicken.

I knew it was not polite to watch her eat it but I could not stop from glancing sideways as she ate that delicious chicken. The aroma was so enticing and mouthwatering that it made my empty stomach growl with hunger. I think she might

∽ Miljenko "Mike" Grgich

have noticed this because she asked me if I would like a piece. Would I? I think I ate not only the meat but the skin and the bones as well. That was certainly one lady I will never forget.

I met other people on the train too, including a businessman who sat next to me for part of the trip. He started to make polite conversation, asking me who I was and where I was going. It was difficult for me to talk when my English was so poor, but I told him I was going to the Yukon to cut trees. Perhaps he noticed I was not enthusiastic.

"Why don't you start your own business?" he asked me.

I didn't have the courage to tell him about my dream to own a winery. I only explained that I did not think I had enough skill to start a business in a new world.

"Why not?" he said. "Owning your own business is the only way to succeed. Work hard. Save your money. Start as cheaply as you can. Get your family to do the jobs. Newcomers can succeed."

Talking to him reminded me of my Papa who had told me, "Learn from everyone you meet." So I put this stranger's words in the back of my mind.

It was snowing when I arrived in Vancouver on the night of February 6, 1956. The train was late, which, though it didn't seem like it at the time, might have been a lucky thing. There was no immigration officer waiting for me at the station, and on such a cold night I did not want to sleep in a train station. I remembered that my nephew, Father Anthony, had said he would leave a message for me. So I went to the station's information desk. Nervously, I just said my name, "Miljenko

Grgić." Yes, there was a message for me. It was: "If you have problems, go to Vancouver College."

This was a Catholic boys' school, and because he was a priest, Father Anthony had connections with them. It was almost midnight when I got to the school. The building was dark but I knocked on the large wooden door anyway and finally someone came to answer the door. The man showed me to a bed on the third floor under the eaves. I was so relieved and grateful to have a place to sleep that night.

In the morning, I was told I could have a job at the school as an assistant dishwasher. I had never done this work before, but then I had never been a lumberjack either, and of the two choices this seemed like the better one.

I set to work. My job was to dry glasses. I picked up one glass and I rubbed it with a towel until it was beautifully polished. Then I noticed that in the time it had taken me to dry just one glass, the other assistant dishwasher had dried a dozen. "Oh no," I thought, "I will lose my job."

I learned to go faster. I believed, and I still believe, that no matter what your job is you have to try to do your best, especially if you are an immigrant. Do your best and you can move up. In six months I was promoted to be a dishwasher and six months later I was a server in the dining room. This surprised me. In Europe you go to college to study to be a waiter, and all I knew was how to dry glasses.

Whatever I had to do to support myself, I kept focusing on my goal to get to California. Now I was much closer, just hundreds of miles away instead of thousands, but I was in

I CONTINUED TO EDUCATE MYSELF BY ATTENDING
ENGLISH CLASS AT VANCOUVER COLLEGE

another country and I still had the problem of getting an American visa. I tried to make the best of my time. When I had free time, I sat in on classes at the college to learn English. While the other guys spent their money going out and having fun, I saved every penny I could.

Canada, too, is where I got my new name. People there told me that no one would be able to pronounce "Miljenko Grgić." At work, someone asked me if I had a nickname. I remembered that my mother would call me Mile (pronounced Mee-leh). So I said, "Mi-le" and the man said back to me, "Mile." I thought this name didn't fit my small stature; a mile, after all, is a big distance. I had overheard someone call another person Mike so I told him, "I will be Mike." Since then I have been known as Mike, and I even Anglicized the spelling of my last name to "Grgich" — with an 'h' at the end so it could be pronounced "ich," which is the sound of the Croatian "ć."

I had been a server for some time when I learned that a new project was opening up. Construction of a paper mill, MacMillan Bloedel, was beginning on Vancouver Island. I got a job as a waiter on the island for the workers during the construction. When the mill was finished, the management began to lay off the workers and soon I was the only one left. I expected to be told I would be terminated but instead, because they knew about my education, I was offered a job in the mill. I would be in charge of paper quality control and it would be my job to collect samples of paper and check them for weight, strength and color. I would have a white coat and my salary would be increased to three dollars an hour. I thought, "I've made it!"

Or had I? Some evenings I would climb the hills and look down at all of the lights of the city. No one was working but still there were so many lights. In the old country, there were no lights at night. I had found freedom in Canada and I had found progress. Was this enough? I was beginning to lose confidence that I would ever get a visa to Paradise. I had been in Germany for eighteen months and in Canada for two and a half years. Was it time to forget about California and make a comfortable life in Vancouver as a quality control officer in a paper factory?

But there, in my room, I still had my fifteen books on winemaking. I had read and reread them while my friends were out playing bocce ball and having a good time. Those books were my capital, the link to my goal. I knew I couldn't give up yet.

My mother had a brother, my Uncle Luka Batinovich, who lived in South Dakota. When he came to Vancouver to visit me, I shared my thoughts with him. Uncle Luka said, "Mike, we are going to get you to the United States."

Together we went to the consulate of the United States in Vancouver. "I have a shop," he said, "and I need Mike to manage this shop for me. He has business experience and education."

The people at the consulate examined my papers. "You have university training in winemaking?" they asked. This was unusual in 1958. Although the wine industry was beginning to grow in California few people had studied winemaking at a college. "You have a better chance to get a visa if you go to

A Glass Full of Miracles

work in the wine industry," they advised me. "That's what you should shoot for."

I told this to Father Anthony, and he came up with an idea. He had connections with the Christian Brothers, who had three wineries in California, in a place called the Napa Valley. He asked their advice. The Brothers told him that I should place an ad seeking a winemaking job in the bulletin of the Wine Institute in San Francisco. That's what I did.

I got a reply from a man named Lee Stewart, who offered me work during the harvest of 1958 at his winery in Napa Valley. The pay was $100 a month and included a room. I was happy and excited. I went to the United States Consulate in Vancouver and showed them that I had a job in Napa Valley. They smiled, congratulated me, and gave me a visa.

I could hardly believe that four years after I had left Croatia with my little cardboard suitcase filled with books, I was finally going to use them in California. After all those months and years of waiting and hoping and doing whatever work I had to do, was my dream really going to come true? I packed my books one more time and bought a ticket for a Greyhound bus that would take me to Paradise — the Napa Valley! And of course, I took my beret with me.

On my way to California I stopped over in Washington State to visit my nephew, Father Anthony, who had been such a great help to me and who was now living in Gig Harbor, Washington. His father was fishing in Port Angeles, which was about two hours away, so Father Anthony took me to his father's boat. Vide had just finished cooking a salmon he caught a few hours earlier. That salmon was the best one I ever ate, even better than the ones in Canada. After such a hearty meal and a glass of wine we started to smile and sing the Croatian song, "Marijana." We were excited about my new adventure and because this was the first time we had met in person. It was my first family reunion in the United States.

After lunch, Father Anthony drove me to see Hoquiam, where he had been born, and then to Aberdeen, where there was a big Croatian community. We visited the Croatian cemetery where Manda, his mother and my sister, had been buried a few years earlier, before I had had the chance to meet her.

I also met my Uncle Matt Batinovich, another one of my mother's brothers, and his family, who also lived in Aberdeen. His wife, Rosa, had sent packages of food and clothing to my family in Desne during and after World War II. She was of Polish origin and was so like a rose, full of beauty, generosity and love.

My Uncle Matt was a barber and he was excited to give me a haircut. He noticed I was balding, so he applied a special lotion he had developed onto my scalp around the area where I had very little hair! He charged customers fifty cents for each application. It was supposed to help grow hair, but I only had the one treatment. I don't know if it worked on others or not.

In Aberdeen I also visited yet another of my mother's brothers, Uncle Joe Batinovich. He was in the insurance business and was also a member of the Aberdeen City Council.

I do not have words strong enough to express the emotions I felt to be with my closest relatives after being alone and living in a world so unfamiliar to me for four years. It was so heartwarming to feel the affection of loved ones, of my family. It was short-lived, but it reinvigorated my spirit. After two delightful and exciting days with my family, I boarded a Greyhound bus again. Finally, I was going to fulfill my dream of going to California. Hooray!

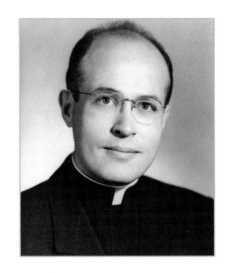

FATHER ANTHONY DOMANDICH, MY NEPHEW. WITHOUT HIS HELP I MIGHT NOT HAVE MADE IT TO NAPA VALLEY.

The bus stopped in many cities I had never heard of. It drove through the state of Oregon. I dozed off and then I felt us stop. The sun had set and it was getting dark. I asked the driver where we were and he replied, "We are in Woodland, California." I looked through the window and to my surprise I saw palm trees.

"Is this really California?" I asked the driver.

He replied, "Yes, this is California."

In my excitement, I think my heart skipped a beat! I couldn't sleep until we reached the last stop. I was the only person left on the bus, but I had reached my destination: St. Helena, California, my Paradise, the Napa Valley.

This historic sign was established in 1950 and continues to welcome millions of visiters to Napa Valley each year.

Chapter 8

Finally Paradise!

When I got off the bus in St. Helena, I felt like I was dreaming. I could hardly believe that after four long years of uncertainty, I was actually stepping into what I called my Paradise. I had mixed emotions, fear as well as happiness. I did not know what the future had in store for me. It was 10:30 at night, and once again, nobody was waiting for me. Once again I was alone in a strange place.

Then I remembered that Mr. Lee Stewart had said to call him when I arrived, and he would come pick me up. I set out in search of a telephone.

St. Helena was a quiet town. The streets were empty of cars and people as I walked. At last I found a public telephone booth and dialed the number Mr. Stewart had sent me. Nervously, I listened to the phone ringing. What if he had forgotten, or worse, had changed his mind?

At last, a man with a gruff voice answered.

"This is Mike Grgich," I said. "Are you Mr. Lee Stewart?"

My relief was great when he replied, "I've been waiting for you," but I was dismayed to hear him say it was too late for him to drive down the mountain. "Better get a room in the hotel," he told me, "I will pick you up in the morning."

Where would I find a hotel? I walked along Main Street until at the corner of Adams Street, I noticed the sign "Hotel" and an arrow pointing down Adams Street. About 100 feet from the corner there was a three-story building with another "hotel" sign. I was surprised because there was no light in the whole building — it was completely dark. I knocked on the entrance door, and then on the front and back windows of the building, calling out loudly to see if someone was inside. I did not find anybody.

Disappointed, I walked back to Main Street and turned right. After a short distance I heard singing and noise in the ground floor of a building and I walked in. I had guessed that it might be a hotel and that the bar was downstairs. Inside I approached the lady behind the front desk and asked, "Is this a hotel?"

She replied, "Yes, this is Hotel St. Helena."

I relaxed and asked if they had an empty room. Politely, she said, "Yes, dear, we have twenty-four empty rooms upstairs. If you pay two dollars, you can go up the stairs and choose any room you like."

I went up the stairs and chose the room closest to the stairs — Room #10. I was so glad to have a bed after the long hours on the bus that I immediately fell asleep.

A Glass Full of Miracles

When I woke up the next morning, I sat on the bed and wondered, "What if Mr. Stewart doesn't pick me up? How many nights then will I have to pay two dollars for a room? What place have I come to and what will my future be here?"

I breathed a sigh of relief when I saw Lee Stewart arrive at the hotel in his pickup truck. He was a tall man, good-looking, quiet and serious. He said little as he drove, and so I had time to look around. I didn't know it then, but I was looking at the place that would become my home for the rest of my life.

Napa Valley, although great in reputation today, is a little place in size: a mere thirty-six miles long, from Calistoga in the north to the southernmost town, American Canyon, which in those days was called Napa Junction. At its widest point it's six miles across. It is flanked on either side by mountain ranges, the Mayacamas range to the west and north, and the Vaca Mountains to the east.

A hundred years before I arrived, other immigrants from Europe had discovered that this small valley had the right climate and soil for growing wine grapes. Newcomers from Italy, France, Germany and Switzerland planted vineyards and built more than one hundred wineries. In the 1880s, the phylloxera epidemic that destroyed the vineyards of Europe came to the valley, but this was not as destructive as Prohibition, the national law passed in 1919 that prohibited making, storing, transporting and selling alcoholic beverages. This law was hard to understand in Europe, where wine was simply a part of life, for people from peasants to royalty.

Prohibition was not a success in the U.S., and in 1934 it

Miljenko "Mike" Grgich

was repealed, but the damage to the wine industry in the Napa Valley had been done. Many wineries had closed, and vineyards had been replanted as orchards or turned into pastures. Only a few vineyards had managed to survive. When I arrived there were only twenty-five wineries in the Napa Valley; throughout the countryside one could see the ruins of many old wineries. They were called "ghost wineries."

America was not a big wine-drinking country in 1958. Beer, whiskey, Coca-Cola and milk were the popular drinks, but interest in wine was beginning to grow, and the valley was waking up, as if from a long sleep. People had slowly been coming to the valley wanting to rebuild the old wineries and learn the art of winemaking. One of them was Lee Stewart.

Lee was a retired businessman with an interest in wine. There was a rumor that he had once been a bootlegger, running liquor during the wild days of Prohibition, but he never said if this was true. In 1943 he had purchased 60 acres with an old winery on Howell Mountain in the eastern Napa hills. He paid $83,000 for the property.

The winery on this property had been built in 1884 by a man named Fulgencio Rossini, who had bought it from a Slovenian man. When Lee bought the property, it still had some old vineyards and prune trees that had been planted in the valley during Prohibition.

It is interesting to me how the name of Lee's winery came about. He had gradually modernized the old winery but could not decide what to name it. One day it occurred to him to write down six potential names on six different slips of paper and put them in a hat.

His only child, a daughter, attended school in Angwin, a mile away from the winery. One day when he took her to school, he brought the hat to her classroom and asked one of her classmates if she would pick one of the slips of paper from the hat, blindfolded. The name she picked was "Souverain," which means "sovereign" or "supreme" in French. So that became his winery's name.

Lee Stewart set out to learn how to make wine from the old-timers, winemakers who had continued to make wine in Napa Valley through the hard times of two world wars, Prohibition, and the Great Depression. But he also wanted to incorporate the best traditions of European winegrowers, combined with the most modern California methods.

He contacted André Tchelistcheff, a Russian immigrant who had studied in France and was now the winemaker for Beaulieu Vineyard. Lee listened to and put on paper every word André told him about making wine. This became a bible for Lee: he followed André's instructions to the letter. His goal was to improve the quality of the wines made in the Napa Valley.

Times were hard at first for Lee Stewart and his wife, a beautiful woman who had been an opera singer. While Lee learned how to make wine, his wife sold eggs and prunes and tried to help out on the farm. One day, while struggling to carry a heavy basketful of prunes to the house, she became so frustrated that she dropped the basket and ran to the house crying. That was the end of her work on the farm!

The Souverain Cellars label

By the time I arrived in 1958, Lee was making some of the best wines in the valley. These included Cabernet Sauvignon, Zinfandel, Green Hungarian, and Johannisberg Riesling. Today Johannisberg Riesling is called simply Riesling because Johannisberg refers to the place in Germany where the wines were originally made. In the early days of winemaking in California, it was customary to give wines the names of the great wines of Europe, such as Burgundy and Champagne, even though these were the names of actual wine regions. Now there is more understanding of the importance of a specific place, and how its individual qualities of soil and climate produce grapes, and therefore wines, that are unique to each appellation. Napa and other regions have become just as important and unique as Burgundy and Champagne. Rather than use the name of another region, they are proud of their own, and so they identify the wines by the grape varieties that the wines are made from, such as Cabernet Sauvignon or Chardonnay.

Souverain Winery was on a remote, lonely site up on the slopes of Howell Mountain. Lee had said some people would be scared out of their wits to try to make wines there, but the place suited him. He showed me the place where I would be living, a little cabin furnished with a bed and a hot plate, but no stove or refrigerator. It was as rustic as the room from my student days in Zagreb, except the bed was a little more comfortable.

On my first night at Souverain winery, Lee and his wife invited me to have dinner with them, and they served two wines, a 1951 Cabernet Sauvignon and a 1954 Zinfandel Lee had made. This was the first time in my life that I had ever tasted a wine that had been aged. In Croatia, we made the wine and drank it all that same year. I had also never tasted wines that were this good. Drinking them, I knew that I was going to have to work very hard to match the quality of the wines that Lee Stewart made.

As I walked back to my cabin, I kept looking at the grapevines that grew near it. I had not seen grapevines since I left Germany so it was like meeting old friends. Some of the vines were especially familiar: they looked like vines from my home in Croatia.

They were Zinfandel vines. I borrowed a book about grapevines from Lee and in it I read that it was known that Cabernet Sauvignon and Chardonnay vines had originated in France, but that no one knew who had brought Zinfandel vines to California or where they had come from. The origin of Zinfandel was a mystery.

It would be many years before I would be able to help prove that Zinfandel had, in fact, originated in my homeland, Croatia. But that first night on Howell Mountain, I was sure it had come from Croatia. Without proof, though, who would believe a poor immigrant like me who hardly spoke English?

That night too, my father's words were with me. Find people you can learn from, he had told me, and I knew that I would learn much from Lee Stewart. And my Papa had said to try to make a new friend every day. Here, so far from my home, when I looked at Zinfandel grapevines I felt like I had found a friend. It came to my mind that I had come to the right place.

Those first days on Howell Mountain, I was not sure if I was in Paradise or the Wild West. Lee Stewart was a sharpshooter and owned a hunting gun. He hunted deer in his vineyard. The eyes of those deer were as bright as flashlights at night! Lee did not eat deer meat so he gave it to his part-time workers.

One evening when I was sitting on the steps of my cabin reading a newspaper to help improve my English, I was startled and looked up to see Lee Stewart standing over me with a shotgun. He fired, and only then did I notice the rattlesnake that had been approaching me, hidden by my newspaper. Lee hit it in the head. I was lucky that Lee was an excellent marksman.

Another danger was fire. After April in Napa Valley, rain falls only rarely, not coming again in earnest until late fall, perhaps October or November. The summers are hot, and especially in the dry eastern hills, once a fire begins it can move swiftly. News came that there was a wildfire on the mountain and the sky turned gray with smoke. The fire came so close I could see its flames. I grabbed my suitcase full of wine books and ran to a nearby reservoir. Fortunately, the fire didn't reach any of us, and my books and I were safe.

Lee Stewart and I worked hard. Cleanliness and quality were Lee's passions. Before the harvest began, we washed and scrubbed all of the equipment, the crusher and the fermenting tanks.

He was a perfectionist, and he worked with only one assistant so he could best control the quality of the wine. This

∽ Miljenko "Mike" Grgich

meant that once harvest began we put in long hours in the vineyards and the winery. One time I came back to my cabin at four o'clock in the morning, weary but also hungry. What could I make quickly so I could eat? I put two eggs to boil on the hotplate and sat down on my bed. In an instant, I was asleep.

I woke up to find smoke filling my room. "Another wildfire!" was my first thought. I leaped from my bed only to find that the water in the pot had boiled away and my eggs were burning. At least this time I did not have to run for the lake.

I worked for Lee Stewart for three months, and at the end of harvest, when the wine was fermenting in its tanks, I knew it was time for me to move on. For one thing, he had no more work for me, but also, it was lonely living up on Howell Mountain and hard to be comfortable in those primitive conditions. Without a car, I was isolated. I had to depend on Lee for rides into St. Helena to buy my food.

I had achieved my goal to find a way to get to California and find work making wine, but I had a greater dream growing inside me: to one day own my own small patch of land in this valley and have my own winery. To do this I knew I had to keep moving forward. I turned to Brother Timothy, the cellarmaster and pioneering winemaker at Christian Brothers, for help and I was offered a job at their winery in St. Helena. I left Lee Stewart and Souverain but I took with me many lessons that I'd learned from my time with him.

My recollection of Lee Stewart is that although he spoke little, he was always moving. He was always looking for the best and was consistent and precise in everything he did. He followed, step-by-step, the process of winemaking that he learned from André Tchelistcheff. In order to avoid mistakes, he did the same thing every year. He would not deviate from what he knew best, and that is how he developed his style and perfected his winemaking skills.

I learned from all the people I worked with in the Napa Valley, and from each I was able to take something to my next job. From Lee Stewart I learned about cleanliness, precision, high quality, passion and the art of winemaking.

He was an artist winemaker. He had an urge to create and what he created was wine. People close to Lee joked that he cared more about his wine than anything else, even his family.

Long after, when I was married, Lee invited us to his home for a dinner party, and I asked my wife to make a cake for Lee. He said, "Mike, you know I can't eat cake. I have problems with my stomach."

One of his friends said, "But at least you don't have any problems with your heart, Lee. That's because you have no heart!"

Lee didn't disagree; he just laughed and poured him a glass of wine.

My recollection is that Lee sold his winery on Howell Mountain in 1972 for $1 million.

Lee died in 1986. The name "Souverain" has changed hands in the course of the years, and it is presently part of the portfolio of Treasure Wine Estates with vineyards in Alexander Valley near Cloverdale.

∽ Miljenko "Mike" Grgich

Today, not many people remember Lee Stewart, maybe because he sold his winery when the Napa wine industry was just starting to come back. But he stood out in those early days. He was an innovator, a member of a small group of winemakers who worked relentlessly to raise the quality of Napa wines. He played an important role in the rebirth of the wine industry in the Napa Valley. Lee Stewart should be remembered and honored by being included in the Vintners Hall of Fame.

The old Souverain Cellars building, which is now Burgess Cellars.

THE CHRISTIAN BROTHERS HISTORIC
GREYSTONE BUILDING, BUILT IN 1889.

Chapter 9

The Christian Brothers

The Christian Brothers have played a significant role in my career. At their suggestion, while I was still in Canada, I had placed an ad in The Wine Institute bulletin in San Francisco for a job as winemaker in California. With a response to that ad in hand, I was granted a visa by the United States Consulate in Canada. And now, I was working for the Christian Brothers.

Coming from Lee Stewart's small operation on Howell Mountain, I had moved to one of the grandest wineries in the valley. It was with a feeling of pride and awe that I walked through the doors of their winery; it was like entering a castle. I sent a picture of the Greystone building to my family in Croatia so that they could see where I was working in America.

Greystone, one of the most famous buildings in the Napa Valley, sits just above Highway 29, north of St. Helena. In the 1880s, a San Francisco businessman named William Bourn, Jr. and his business partner, Everett Wise, hired the architectural firm of Percy and Hamilton to design this grand building. Bourn's vision was to form a cooperative in Napa Valley and establish a one million gallon winery and cellar where winemakers could store their wine. Then, they could sell the wine on the free market instead of going through San Francisco distributors who manipulated the market. Among the conditions set by Mr. Bourn was that only quality grapes and wine would be received and allowed to be stored.

The latest technology and best materials, such as Portland cement and the local "tufa," a variety of limestone found in the area, were used in the construction, which ran from 1886 to 1889. The final cost amounted to $250,000, a huge amount in those days! It had already had several owners by the time the Christian Brothers purchased the building in 1950. Today it is the home of the California campus of the Culinary Institute of America.

The Brothers are a teaching order, and in 1882 they began selling brandy out of their location in Martinez to support their education programs. All throughout Prohibition, they were able to continue making their sacramental wines and brandy. In the 1930s they moved to the Napa Valley by purchasing 338 acres on Mt. Veeder, which included an old stone winery, and called it Mont La Salle. When they bought Greystone, they moved and expanded their winemaking operations there but kept Mont Las Salle as administrative headquarters and a conference and retreat center — as well as a vineyard source. They made still and sparkling wines, along with brandy and Port-style wines.

A Glass Full of Miracles

Brother Timothy Diener had been a science teacher, but he had a change in career when in 1935 he became involved in the Christian Brothers winery. He began as a chemist, and later had the added responsibility of supervising the vineyards. He was promoted to be supervisor of the winery and eventually he became vice-president of the winery corporation.

Brother Timothy was a remarkable man: his mental sharpness and business acumen were admirable. He shared his knowledge with other winemakers and became one of the forces in reviving the wine industry in the Napa Valley. He provided financial assistance to the Napa Valley Vintners Association (now Napa Valley Vintners) in the late 1940s.

He also practiced his vows of poverty and humility. He was not materialistic, but he loved plants, especially orchids. And he was a corkscrew collector. His collection must have been one of the biggest in the world — 1,100 in all!

Christian Brothers was the largest winery in the valley in 1959 when I began working there, and Brother Timothy was the winemaker. Christian Brothers made excellent Cabernet Sauvignon and a well-liked white wine called Chateau La Salle. This wine was made from Johannisberg Riesling grapes with residual sugar of five percent, a soft wine perfect for hors d'oeuvres or just a glass by itself anytime.

I remember that whenever Brother Timothy had meetings with winemakers in Napa Valley he began with a prayer. One of them was, "O Great God, Creator of a Universe so immense that our most brilliant scientists, capable of sending men to the moon and bringing them back home again, are unable to measure its extent, You are the same God who made microscopic yeast cells that convert grape juice into wine."

There were no positions as winemaker or wine chemist open, and so I went to work in the sparkling wine department. I worked on the third floor of the Greystone building and did everything related to making sparkling wine — bottling, production and shipping.

This was not a job I wished to do forever, yet it was still an opportunity to learn many things. It was from the Christian Brothers, for example, that I learned how to open a wine bottle without a corkscrew: you wrap the bottom of the bottle in a cloth and hit it gently against the ground until the cork works its way out of the bottle. Try it — it works!

Another thing I learned was how a large winery operated. Mr. Auguste Pirio was the manager of Greystone. He was a humane man whose first concern was safety for all the employees. Every day we would meet and go over our daily job duties. He would walk through the winery, and if he saw anyone running or doing anything dangerous, he would stop them. Even if you objected, saying, "But this way is faster," he would not allow it if it was not safe. He cared about every employee and held a picnic each year for workers and their families.

I can only say good things about the Christian Brothers. They treated everyone with respect, and if you had a job there, you could stay for your entire career. Still, the question nagging me was how to move forward. Although it was a fine place to work, after a few months I knew there was little

BROTHER TIMOTHY DEMONSTRATING ONE OF THE
CORKSCREWS FROM HIS FAMOUS COLLECTION.

possibility of advancement. The Christian Brothers held most of the important jobs at the winery and I knew it was not my destiny to become a Brother.

What should my next step be? All around me I could see wineries that other immigrants had built. Across the street from Christian Brothers was Charles Krug, the first commercial winery that had been built in the Napa Valley, in 1861. It was now owned by another immigrant, Cesare Mondavi, who had bought it in the 1930s. Next door was Beringer Winery, built by two brothers from Germany in 1875. Then, as now, many of the people who had come to the Napa Valley to build their dream of owning a winery had brought with them money they had earned in another place, doing other work. What possibilities were there for me, who had arrived with nothing except a suitcase full of books?

The Christian Brothers winery had a wine chemist named Dick Dettman who was doing all the analyses and quality control. He had worked there for ten years, and I asked him if he needed an assistant. He told me he kept everything under control and he intended to work there for about twenty more years. Still it was a useful conversation because I learned from him that there was going to be a one-week seminar on "Dry Table Wine" at the University of California in Davis. With his help, I was able to sign up for the seminar.

When I arrived in the town of Davis, I found a nice motel. The receptionist gave me a form to fill out. I asked, "How much does a room cost per night?"

She replied, "$2.50 a night."

I was puzzled that in Davis it cost $2.50 while I had only paid $2 per night six months earlier in St. Helena. I could not help but ask the receptionist why the discrepancy. She smiled and said, "Why don't you go to St. Helena then and sleep there for $2?"

The idea that the cost of things was not the same throughout California was a big surprise for me, because in Communist Yugoslavia prices were controlled by the government and so they were uniform wherever you went.

The professors at UC Davis had a different approach than those at the University of Zagreb in Croatia. At Davis they would start the course with a story to make the students feel relaxed.

For example, one day a professor began with this story: An old farmer was lying in his bed, feeling very sick. He felt so terrible that he told his two sons that he was dying. When they heard this, the older son told his younger brother, "When Father dies, we will divide the property. The land that never floods is mine, and the rest of the land, the part that floods, will be divided between us, half for you and half for me."

While the brothers were discussing the division of the property, the old man could hear their conversation. He closed his eyes and pretended to be dead. The younger son immediately noticed that his father had closed his eyes so he knelt by his bed and started to pray for his father's soul. The older son was not sure if his father was really dead so he approached the bed and put his head close to his father's head. When the old man felt his older son's head close to his, he

My professors and fellow students at a seminar at U.C. Davis. I'm sitting in the front row, the fourth one from the right.

blurted out with a strong voice, 'BOO!' Since the father now knew what his older son was really like, he decided to leave his entire property to his younger son.

On another occasion the same professor started the class with an important subject, "The Future of California Wineries." He said, "In the future wineries will be designed in circles, with spokes radiating out from a central hub. Inside, in a circle next to the wall, there will be stainless steel jacketed tanks with temperature control. In one tank there will be alcohol, in another acid, in the next there will be water with aromas and flavors, next there will be color, next to it there will be tannin, and so on.

"In the middle of the winery there will be a computer — a computer that will make a 'Master Blend' by allocating each compound into the central tank. A perfect wine!"

Five years later in Los Angeles I heard the same professor talk about the same subject, "The Perfect Wine." This time he said, "Some day we will have a 'perfect wine', but it will be produced by an artist winemaker."

This, I felt, was a better statement than the one I had heard from him at UC Davis.

One Saturday the foreman of the bottling line invited me to her home for lunch. She picked me up and we drove to her house on Madrona Street in St. Helena. She was a lovely lady with two sons, one daughter, and a husband, and I saw that a total of five cars and a pickup were parked in front of the house and in the garage. I asked her why there were so many cars. She replied, "Each of us works in a different place, so we each need a car." It was a typical American family where each member had his own vehicle, but I had never seen such a thing before.

Seeing this family with six cars reminded me of an "Artistic Photography Exhibit" I had seen in Croatia. To me, the most interesting and artistic photograph was the one that came from America — a picture of a busy street full of cars so close together that they were almost touching one another. It was titled, "Arteriosclerosis of the Street." I thought that it was a scene that was put together just for the photograph, but when I came to America I realized that it was for real — I now knew why people said that the only free parking space in the USA was the Los Angeles freeway!

I was learning about life in America, although I knew I was not living like a real American. I did not own a car; I took a bus to Davis. In St. Helena I rented a room that did not have a refrigerator or a stove, and I walked to work each day. In fact, the only things I had bought for myself were a little knife that I used for cooking and eating, a small spoon and a hot plate.

When my brother-in-law Vide came to visit me, he was shocked at the way I was living. "Mike," he said, "you are working, earning a salary. You don't have to live in such poor conditions."

My habit to save money and to never go into debt was strong, but he insisted I had to improve my life. We looked at houses for sale in St. Helena, and I agreed to buy the cheapest one, 1212 Edwards Street: the cost was $8,500, and Vide loaned me $2,500 for the down payment — these were enormous amounts of money for me.

The house was in bad shape. One of the first things I had to do was to repair the floor, which rippled and buckled. I had to go under the house and try to push up the floorboards with a small jack, and then come up to check to see if it was now flat.

Vide bought me a refrigerator; it was the first time in my life I had owned such a thing. He wanted to buy a garbage can too, and I asked him, "Why?" I still followed my habits from my old country, where we didn't have garbage because we used everything that we cooked and we burned any paper wrappers in the yard.

As Vide left to return to Washington State, he remarked that my life was better now, but inside I was still filled with doubts. I was now thirty-six years old. If I had stayed in Croatia, I would most surely have been married by now; I would have children. I would have my sisters and brothers and their children and many friends around me. Instead, I was thousands of miles away from my home, and I was alone. What chance, I wondered, would I have to find a wife, a short guy like me, who could not speak good English and did not own a car? I can tell you that, even though I now owned my own house, many nights the pillow on my bed was wet with tears as I worried what would become of me; where was my life in my new surroundings leading me to?

In the evenings after work, I took an English class at the St. Helena Elementary School. On a wall of the room was a large sign that read, "PUSH OR PULL — If you cannot do either, get out of the way."

∽ Miljenko "Mike" Grgich

This was a brutal thought, but it was true. And in my case, because I could not go back, the only way was forward. And this is how I met André Tchelistcheff.

On the back porch of 1212 Edwards St., proudly holding bottles of Christian Bros. wine, with my cousins Mary Stabio (far right) and Helen Sutich (on the railing wearing pearls).

ANDRÉ TCHELISTCHEFF

Chapter 10

André Tchelistcheff

Nervously I listened to the phone ringing. Would he answer? Would he have the time to talk to me?

I had heard the name André Tchelistcheff many times since my arrival in the Napa Valley. I knew he was the best winemaker for the best winery in the region. His wines were considered the best in America. He was called "The Dean of California Winemakers," who would teach winemaking to those who asked for his help. Lee Stewart had been one of his students.

When I thought about this man, I remembered my father's advice: "Be associated with people who know more than you and learn from them." I knew that I had to meet this formidable man, Tchelistcheff, to see if he could help me too.

With that in mind I had gained the courage to call André Tchelistcheff's office to ask for an appointment to see him. His secretary answered my call. She was sympathetic and pleasant to speak with, so I asked if I could leave my telephone number for Mr. Tchelistcheff to return my call when he had time. Then I waited.

What gave me hope was that André, like me, was an immigrant and a refugee who had fled Communism. He was born in Russia in 1901 to a family who had been landowners for many generations. When the Russian Revolution came in 1917, André fought in the White Army before he fled the country to be reunited with his family, who had escaped to Yugoslavia.

He led a wandering life until he won a scholarship to study agricultural technology, first in Czechoslovakia and then at the Institut Pasteur and the Institut National Agronomique in France. He studied enology, fermentation and microbiology. When Prohibition ended in America in 1938, Georges de Latour, the owner of Beaulieu Vineyard winery in the Napa Valley, traveled to France in search of the best winemaker he could find to improve the quality of his wines. He was told that the person he was looking for was André Tchelistcheff.

Georges de Latour was also an immigrant. He was born in Bordeaux in 1856 and came to San Francisco as a young man. Trained as a chemist, he made his fortune by manufacturing cream of tartar from the skins of grapes, and then in 1900 he decided he wanted a winery in the Napa Valley. The story goes that when his wife, Fernande, first saw the site in Rutherford, she exclaimed, "*Quel beau lieu!*" — what a beautiful place — and that is how the winery got its name, Beaulieu.

A clever businessman, de Latour had been able to keep

his winery operating during Prohibition because he had permission from the bishop in San Francisco to make wine for the Catholic Church. An even smarter business decision was to hire André Tchelistcheff and bring him to the Napa Valley.

In those days, the best restaurants were not serving wines from California. Everyone wanted French wines, and Georges de Latour wanted to make wines that were as good as the French. André brought the knowledge, techniques and traditions of grape growing and winemaking from France. He set out to raise the standards of production in every aspect, even including sanitation. When I arrived in Napa, the Georges de Latour Private Reserve Cabernet Sauvignon that André Tchelistcheff was making was considered to be the best wine made in the United States.

So, you might understand why I was anxious about calling André Tchelistcheff, and how happy I was when he called me back. "Come and talk to me," he said

When I got off the bus from St. Helena at Beaulieu Vineyards in Rutherford, I was astonished to see that this great man was even shorter than I was. He had enormous thick eyebrows. My greatest surprise, however, came after I greeted him in broken English: he answered me in perfect Croatian! For me to meet a man who was not only short and an immigrant like me, but to hear him speak to me in my own language was a miracle.

He told me that during the years after he left Russia, he joined a traveling circus. When the circus was in Croatia, he learned some of the language. He said that he sang and danced

In the laboratory at Beaulieu Vineyard

in the circus, and this was certainly something to imagine.

We had a nice visit. I told him that I was working for Christian Brothers but there was little chance of advancement because they had only one wine chemist and one winemaker who would never leave. He nodded; he understood.

I returned to Christian Brothers and several weeks went by. Then I got another telephone call from André. "My wine chemist is ill," he told me. "Would you like to try working here?"

Another miracle had happened!

There was one condition: I was on trial for two months. I always tried to do my best at every job I ever had, whether it was dishwashing or winemaking, but never had I worked so hard as I did those two months at Beaulieu, when my future depended on my performance. I knew this was the place I wanted to be. Joe Heitz had worked for André for six years and now his winery, Heitz Cellars, was making some of the finest wines in the valley.

I had no car, and my work was to begin at eight o'clock in the morning. I took the six o'clock Greyhound bus from St. Helena to Rutherford to be sure I'd be on time. I arrived at Beaulieu Vineyard at 7 a.m.

As my first task, André assigned me twenty-five wine samples to analyze for their levels of alcohol, sugar, acid, SO_2 and pH. I had not done this work before and when I said I might need help to run each analysis, he gave me a book to read. The instructions in the book were very confusing, but I read through it quickly and then I went to the lab to see if I could find anything there that would help me begin my task.

◈ Miljenko "Mike" Grgich

The lab was modern, with a white Formica counter and equipment for each of the many steps of each analysis. There was a machine for measuring alcohol, one for measuring the color of wines, a pH meter, an oxygen meter, a tall steamer to sterilize juice and utensils.

I found some previous lab records and studied them to see how to proceed. I made my own tests, which I then checked against prior tests and recorded the results. Step by step, I finally finished the job in one week. When I gave the results to André, he was pleased. This was a great relief but my work was only beginning.

During those two trial months I kept coming to work at seven in the morning. My father's words were with me every day. "Learn something new each day; do something better each day." It was as if he were coming to work with me each morning.

I counted the days and finally the two months were over. When I went to work that day I was as nervous as I had been the first time I came to Beaulieu Vineyards. "Mr. Tchelistcheff," I began as soon as I saw him, "may I humbly ask you — "

"What is it, Mike?" he interrupted. "I am very busy today."

"My trial," I said, "my two months — "

"What?" he asked. " Oh that. Yes, of course, you made it. You have a job. And I'll give you a raise."

I got a raise of 25 cents per hour, making my hourly pay $3.25. I felt like a king; this raise told me that I had a future in wine.

Working with André Tchelistcheff was the best thing

that could have happened to me. He was intelligent and highly educated about vines and wines, and he was relentless in his search to improve his wines by constantly learning, researching, reading enology books and trade journals and following progress in the world of wines and vineyards. He read French trade journals and kept up with what was being done in Europe. He always had a connection with France.

For André, progress was based on research — testing ideas, recording results and trying again. He taught more winemakers in the world than any man of his time. For the nine years that I worked for him, I absorbed his wisdom like a thirsty sponge.

There is more to be said about André. He was not just a good wine man, but a good human being. He had a good Slavic heart, a warm and welcoming heart.

We worked well together. André liked being in the vineyards more than in the winery, and this was where he could usually be found. One day he looked sternly at me and said, "Mike, because I spend most of my time in vineyards I want you to be my eyes and ears inside the winery. Tell me immediately whatever you see or hear that is not good so I can take care of it immediately. You will help me and the winery to function at the highest level possible."

When he asked me to bring him samples of red wines, he would also ask for a sample of white wine with high acid. He would activate his taste buds by tasting the white wine first. Red wines can close up the taste buds, while crisp white wines wake them up, almost as if they had been sleeping.

☙ Miljenko "Mike" Grgich

Because we were both Slavs and shared the same culture and values, we understood each other. Sometimes we spoke Croatian. We both wanted the highest standards in everything, including the lowly job of sanitation. When I showed André the larvae of fruit flies clustered around the bungholes of barrels, he said that I would be his quality control officer as well as his chemist. After this I inspected every barrel and tank that was filled with wine.

To tell the truth, I preferred being in the vineyards too. It is important to know your vines, like you know your children, to listen to them and hear what they tell you, but the most important responsibility of a winemaker is quality control — carefully looking after every aspect of quality in the wine, in the winery and in the vineyard. My education at Beaulieu Vineyard was tremendous during the nine years I was there, and it was this experience that helped me later to formulate my winemaking methodology and philosophy.

During these busy and important years at Beaulieu Vineyard, another important thing happened: I got married.

I had wondered how I would ever find a wife. I envied my friend Hans Kornell, another immigrant, who had married a schoolteacher, a smart and educated woman. How I wished the same for myself!

I was growing more accustomed to American ways, but still I knew it would be best for me to be with someone from my own country, someone who understood and could share Croatian ways, our foods, our traditions. I remembered a woman from Split whom I had met many years earlier through her younger sister, in a somewhat unusual way. Here's what happened:

I was traveling on the ferryboat from Split to Ploče, by Metković, when I noticed a young girl traveling all by herself. We struck up a conversation.

"Is someone going to meet you?" I asked her.

"Oh yes," she said. "My best friend from school. I am going to Desne to visit her."

"How do you know she will be there?" I asked.

"Because I sent her a telegram yesterday telling her when I would arrive."

"She won't be there," I told her.

Later I learned that she was beginning to feel uncomfortable at this point — who was this strange man saying such things? — but I had said that because I knew that it would take at least three days for a telegram to get to Desne. When we arrived, I was right. Her friend wasn't there.

"What is her name?" I asked this young girl.

"Jelica Jeramaz," she said.

"Well, that is my niece!" I exclaimed. "So I can take you to her."

So all was well. Vjeka Čizmić and my niece Jelica had been best friends at school in Split. This incident was the beginning of a friendship between the two families as well. I met Vjeka's older sister Tatjana, and she was a fine woman. But I had to leave her behind when I fled from Zagreb.

∽ Miljenko "Mike" Grgich

Now these many years later I thought of Tatjana, and I learned from my family that she too had never gotten married. I wondered, would she be so brave as to come to America and marry me?

I asked her this in a letter. She said yes, and in 1963 I was able to bring Tatjana to California. We were married right after harvest at St. Helena Catholic Church, with André and the Marquis and Madame du Pins in attendance.

Tatjana was a good wife to me during our thirty years of marriage. She supported my work, my struggles, and my dreams. She also gave me the greatest gift, my daughter Violet, who was born in 1965. The name Violet is the English version of Ljubica, after my sister who was like a mother to me after my father and mother passed away. Although our marriage ended, Tatjana, who lives in St. Helena, remains my friend, and I honor her for all that she brought into my life.

At Beaulieu, we made wine in the classical French style, but we added two innovations that André knew were important. The first had to do with malolactic fermentation, something that no one except André knew much about in those days. This is the process by which malic acid, which is present in freshly pressed grape juice called "must," is converted by a special bacteria into lactic acid, which is a weaker acid. This process reduces the total acid in wine and raises the pH. Wines become softer and smoother.

Malolactic fermentation can happen naturally, but we began investigating the possibility of inoculating wine with the necessary bacteria to start and therefore control the process.

On my wedding day at St. Helena Catholic Church, with Marquis du Pins and André Tchelistcheff. My nephew Father Anthony Domandich officiated.

Tatjana and I

By 1962, André was able to introduce malolactic fermentation in Beaulieu Vineyard's red wines by inoculation.

I had been working six months in the lab with twelve different French bacteria cultures, and a few from UC Davis. Finally we chose one that was from UC Davis, called "Davis, ML 34." We started a culture in the laboratory, induced that culture into all the lots of red wine at Beaulieu, and were able to ferment every single one of them in two months. That was quite an achievement! Before this, a few wineries had been doing this in their labs and in their cellars on a small scale, but this was the first time it was done in an industrial way in a large California winery. André and I were able to present this process at a seminar at UC Davis with an audience of more than one hundred wine professionals from the United States, France, Germany and Italy.

An incident that I will remember forever happened to me during experimentation with the malolactic starter in the laboratory. We began the starter in a one-gallon jug, and after we saw that it was working, we transferred the starter to five-gallon demijohns so we could inoculate the big stainless steel fermentation tanks in the winery.

When I saw that the malolactic starter was bubbling away in the five-gallon demijohn, I lifted it and carried it on my back to the cellar to dump the starter into the red wine tank. The demijohn was so heavy and difficult to carry that on the way to the cellar my legs crumbled underneath me. I fell on the cement floor, the five-gallon demijohn fell on top of me and broke, and the starter spilled all over me and then spread

◌ Miljenko "Mike" Grgich

in a big puddle on the floor.

Fortunately I had another five-gallon demijohn starter that the cellarmaster, Ernie Degarde, was able to dump into the red wine tank. When that tank of wine went through malolactic fermentation, samples from it were used to inoculate all the other red wine tanks. In one month, all the red wine tanks went through the first large-scale industrially induced malolactic fermentation in a winery.

The wine had not only survived but was a great success, but I, however, was hospitalized in Santa Rosa for two months as a result of the accident. I can still picture in my mind the day my little daughter Violet brought me a beautiful red rose when she and Tatjana came to visit me in the hospital.

At this time, the traditional method employed to filter wines right before they were bottled used asbestos as a filtering agent. Because this filtration was not calibrated, small amounts of yeast and bacteria would sometimes slip through the asbestos and get trapped in the bottle. When this happened, the bottled wine would be spoiled.

This problem led to our second innovation at Beaulieu, Millipore micro-filtration that was calibrated. This was a very fine filter that trapped yeast and bacteria that would otherwise slip through asbestos filters. The Millipore filtration system, which was used for making medicines sterile, was superior to anything else in use in winemaking. With the introduction of Millipore filtration, we were able to develop and install a double filtration system. First, we put wine through the traditional asbestos filtering to take away most of the impurities, bacteria and yeast; and second, we put the wine through the microscopic system that was the calibrated Millipore filtration.

Before bottling, the Millipore filter was checked using gas pressure. If eighteen pounds of pressure in the filter would not produce any bubbles in the water at the bottom of the filter, it meant that no yeast or bacteria could pass through. The same test was done after filtration to be sure that no breakage happened during filtration.

Since then, Beaulieu Vineyard never had any problems with yeast or bacteria in their bottled wines because their wines were finally microbiologically stable. They had a longer and happier shelf life — and the wines were better. This idea was soon adopted by many other wineries. It was almost a miracle!

We also worked on another important process: cold fermentation of white wine. For wines to be in perfect balance they must be harvested when the aromas, flavors, sugar, acid and tannins are at their optimum, and all of these must be preserved. Most aromas are volatile gases that escape in the high temperatures produced naturally during fermentation. To prevent these aromas from escaping, the temperature has to be maintained at a cooler level. Cold fermentation is one way to achieve this. The process was not new, but it was necessary to have a machine called a "cooler" and most wineries didn't have one. We got a cooler and supervised carefully as the wine was pumped through it and emerged at lower temperature. Usually the wine would be cooled to 45 to

↜ Miljenko "Mike" Grgich

50 degrees Fahrenheit. When the wine warmed up, it would be pumped through again to cool it.

We also worked on testing strains of yeast from all over the world. When you fermented only with yeasts naturally present on the grapes, there were so many strains you could never be sure which strain would dominate and what character your finished wine would have. Commercial yeasts were used to ensure consistency and quality, and we ended up with two favorite strains: French White for red wines, and a Riesling strain for white wines.

We also started using paper chromatography to control the results of malolactic fermentation, which we learned from UC Davis. The acids present in wines are tartaric, malic and lactic. Each acid showed up on the paper as a line, the heaviest acid being tartaric, then malic, with lactic as the lightest. When no malic acid appeared but you saw lactic instead, you knew that malolactic fermentation was finished. Another technique for preventing malolactic fermentation was using fumaric acid in certain doses. This would not allow the malolactic bacteria to grow. Cool temperatures below 60 degrees Fahrenheit would also keep malolactic bacteria from growing.

How did Napa winemakers progress so quickly in improving the quality of their wines? Not only were we all actively working to find better ways to make wine, but we were also sharing everything we were doing, learning from one another, and that helped everyone move forward. "When the tide rises, all ships rise with it," was the philosophy of leaders like André Tchelistcheff and Robert Mondavi. This spirit of generosity and innovation was like what I had known in my small village of Desne, where everyone helped their neighbors whenever they could and learned from each other.

Three elements helped this process. First was the research being done at the University of California at Davis. Wine grape growing was not so sophisticated in those days. Research from UC Davis was beginning to guide growers as to where to plant different varieties for the best results. They were also investigating questions such as how much water the vines needed and which chemicals were necessary to protect the crop.

The other elements were the two groups who shared all of these discoveries: the Napa Valley Vintners and the Wine Technical Group.

The Wine Technical Group, composed of winemakers, met monthly at dinner to taste wines from different wineries and to listen to a guest speaker from UC Davis. Most of the dinners were at Vern's Copper Chimney, which was just about the only restaurant in St. Helena. We would talk about our problems, how the season was going and improvements in bottling.

The Napa Valley Vintners were mostly owners; the group had started in the 1940s, and also met once a month, for lunch. The philosophy behind the Napa Valley Vintners dictated that at these lunch meetings they would look into each others' eyes — that they would be friends instead of competitors.

André took me with him to the monthly lunch meetings of the Napa Valley Vintners, which was a great source of

∽ Miljenko "Mike" Grgich

knowledge and comradeship. There were about ten to twenty members of the Vintners at this time, and the Vintners' secretary, Mr. Beard, organized the monthly meetings. At these meetings you would find men like Brother Timothy or Roy Raymond, who worked at Beringer and later started Raymond Winery. They would talk about business and legal questions as well as winemaking and grape growing. We would taste the wines and share our ideas and innovations. There would be discussions about all kinds of things that in other industries were considered secrets, but the idea was that we would come together to benefit everyone individually and as a group. This was important because before the creation of the Napa Valley Vintners, everyone tried to promote his own wine by putting everyone else down. But when you had to look at one another face-to-face, across a table, you couldn't do that. It was a smart beginning for cooperation, and helped the wine business advance more quickly.

Another reason that the wine industry in Napa Valley also advanced quickly was because it was so far behind Europe, everyone knew they had to catch up. They would have talks by UC Davis professors every now and then, and each month one winery was assigned to bring its wines for the meeting. Tasting each other's wines helped improve the quality of the wines. We started out by trying to find the flaws in the wine. There were so many flaws in the wines, such as iron, protein and copper in the sediment, and so many bad wines on the market, that the best tasters in those days were the ones who could detect the most deficiencies in wine. Both groups, the Vintners and the Wine Technical Group, would then go to UC Davis with their problems and ask the professors if they could solve the problem with research, and if a larger winery did research it would share the results with the other wineries. This was the progress that was made in those days. The 1960s, '70s and '80s were the years of the great wine evolution in California; I came to the valley at the right time to be part of this historic move forward. Today, American wine has been so elevated that the best tasters are the ones who can taste the good and positive things in wine since the flaws have been eliminated.

Our knowledge has improved, but sometimes I observe that today the unity in the Napa Valley that existed in those early days has diminished, and the fellowship that helped us finally achieve the quality we were searching for is less apparent.

No matter how far we advanced technically, there was one aspect of winemaking we could not control then and still cannot control today. It is the most powerful one of all, Mother Nature. Wind, rain, sun and frost: it is Mother Nature who decides what we get each year.

One of the biggest threats to the grape crop in the Napa Valley is frost. The most dangerous time for frost is in spring after bud break, when the vines wake up from their winter sleep and the first signs of green appear. A severe frost after bud break can threaten an entire crop. On those cold nights we did everything to protect the vines. The vineyards in those days were in much more danger than today because the ways to deal with frost were somewhat primitive.

Let me describe the challenges of the year 1961, to

illustrate how Mother Nature can impact the vineyards. It is said that bad things happen in threes, and that is what happened in 1961. First, the season began with eighteen days of frost in a row. This meant eighteen days of very little sleep, where we worked in the winery by day and in the vineyards by night trying to save the grapes. We would light fires in smudge pots and sometimes burn tires to warm the air. We would go home looking like chimney sweeps.

One night all of Napa Valley was lit up with smudge pots, and the air was full of smoke. The daughter of Georges and Fernande de Latour had married the Marquis de Pins and they now owned Beaulieu. That night Madame de Pins came driving into the vineyard in her Cadillac. "I've come to help you," she said. "I couldn't sleep. It seems the whole valley is on fire."

I said, "Madame, it is kind of you to want to help but I don't think you can light smudge pots. But it's really cold out here, and if you could make coffee for the workers, that would warm them up."

She said, "Mike, to be honest, I have never made coffee in my whole life."

I had forgotten that she belonged to French aristocracy. Her house had sixteen rooms and she had four servants. I said, "Then Madame, you had better go home. It is freezing and you will get all smudged up here." We would have to do without coffee.

Although the primary crop was severely damaged as a result of the frost, there was plenty of second crop in 1961. This might seem like a good thing, but this was, in a way, the second bad thing that happened that year. This is because the quality and quantity of second crop grapes is not as high as first crop. So, because that year's vintage contained more second crop than first crop, we harvested only 13,000 tons instead of the usual 20,000. But we survived.

Third, at the end of the year it rained. There simply was not enough sunshine for the grapes to mature. I remember that we picked Sauvignon Blanc with a sugar content of 16 percent. We fortified the wine with 90 percent alcohol to reach the normal alcohol level in wine. The ground was so wet that the tractors could not be driven in the vineyards, so the boxes of grapes were pulled out of the vineyards on slats, by horses.

Much has changed since then. Today, to combat the threat of frost, we have wind machines instead of smudge pots; sometimes water sprinklers are used, just like I had seen in Germany.

By 1966 I felt I had finally achieved success in my work and in my life. I was invited to join The American Society for Enology and Viticulture. I owned a house in Napa. I had a wife and a daughter. "What is next?" I asked myself.

André Tchelistcheff never owned his own winery or put his name on a bottle, and many people asked him why, for he certainly should have succeeded. His reply was always that because he had lived through a revolution, he was content and happy to work at Beaulieu. He knew what it was like to lose everything. He did not want that to happen again. "I am too European to take a risk," he would say.

André is still well revered today. He is called "the father

of modern American wine-making," or simply "The Maestro." His gifts to the Napa Valley and the world of wine are known throughout the world, and he certainly deserves to have a monument dedicated to him.

Within a couple of years, André began to think of retiring. But he had a son, Dmitri, and I knew that he would take his father's place one day. Where should I go?

I was thinking of these things one evening at Beaulieu as I watched the handyman's children playing in the dirt. I knew how hard this man worked for his family and it reminded me of my home, my father and mother, and my brothers and sisters. I knew that this man, José Brambila, thought of me as a success. I wore a white coat and worked in a laboratory. I had authority and responsibility. I wondered if he knew that his children could achieve this too?

I said to him, "You should try to send at least one of your children to study enology at UC Davis to become educated and become a winemaker. This you could do."

Years later one of his sons became one of the first Mexican-Americans to graduate from the winemaking program at UC Davis. Little did I know, when I advised José Brambila on the education of his children, that one day his son Gustavo would come to me for a job, and would work with me at Grgich Hills Cellar for twenty-three years. Little did I know that one day Gustavo Brambila and I would become the owners of our own wineries.

No, at that moment all I had was a dream, the same dream I had had for so many years. It was still alive inside me: to own my own land and winery. I was telling this man to try to move his family ahead, and I knew deep inside that it was also time for me to take the next step forward. And so I made an appointment to see Robert Mondavi.

BEAULIEU VINEYARDS CIRCA 1960

A Glass Full *of* Miracles

Putting Down Roots

The ship Italia, which brought me from Germany to the New World.

My friend Marko Đaja is on the left standing with his friend in front of the paper factory where I worked in Vancouver, British Columbia.

My Uncle Matt Batinovich and his lovely wife Rosa

Praying at my sister Manda's grave in Aberdeen in 1958

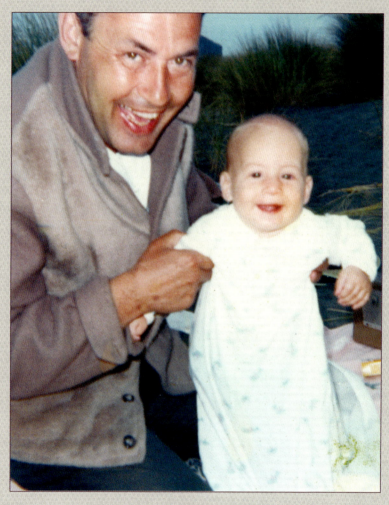

My daughter Violet's smile is almost as big as mine.

Vide playing accordion for Violet

In the back yard of 1212 Edwards St. with my young daughter Violet holding my favorite flower, a red rose.

Tatjana tending our side yard "vineyard" at 1212 Edwards St.

Robert Mondavi

Chapter 11

Robert Mondavi

Robert Mondavi became my employer for four years, and my friend for life. In 1968, his name was not yet widely famous, but in a valley as small as Napa, I knew of him, just as he knew of me.

He was ten years older than I was, and he had just built his own winery in Oakville, which lies between the towns of Rutherford and Yountville. Robert Mondavi had learned about wine from his father, Cesare. His parents had emigrated from the Marche region of Italy, which is just across the Adriatic Sea from Croatia. They had first lived in Minnesota, where Robert was born in 1913, then moved to Lodi in the Central Valley of California. There Cesare Mondavi had a wholesale business shipping grapes to the east coast. It was Robert who had persuaded his father to move to St. Helena, where the Mondavi family first bought part ownership in the Sunny Saint Helena Winery and then, in 1943, the Charles Krug Winery, the historic winery across the street from the

Miljenko "Mike" Grgich

Christian Brothers Winery.

Cesare worked together with his two sons, Peter and Robert, with Peter as winemaker and Robert in charge of sales and marketing. The brothers, however, had different ideas about many things, from their styles of living to making and selling wine. Peter was more cautious, while Robert was the driver, always charging ahead. The whole valley knew of the fistfight between the brothers, which had started over a mink coat that Robert had bought his wife and ended with Robert leaving the family business to start his own.

The Robert Mondavi Winery was the first big winery to be built in the Napa Valley since Prohibition. We didn't know then that Robert Mondavi had started a golden age for new wineries in the Napa Valley. When I went to meet him in 1968, his winery was only two years old.

I was very much charmed by Robert Mondavi's new winery. No other winery in the valley looked like it. Instead of the solid stone buildings that the winemakers from the 19th century had built, Robert had hired an architect to design a winery in the style of the old California missions. His winery was graceful and elegant, fresh and clean, and filled with the newest equipment, stainless steel tanks and French oak barrels.

We sat on a bench outside his new winery and talked. Robert was like a vacuum cleaner, sucking information out of me. He wanted to know everything that I was doing at Beaulieu, everything about André Tchelistcheff and our work together. He said to me, "Mike, if you come to work for me, I will make of you a little André Tchelistcheff." The word "little" did not bother me. I knew what a great man André Tchelistcheff was. I also knew that my time of working with André at Beaulieu was coming to an end. I took the job.

Robert Mondavi was a man with a thousand ideas but one goal: to raise the quality of Napa wines to be as good as the best wines in the world, the French. He said that only the best would survive and he intended to be the best.

The atmosphere at his new winery was completely different from Beaulieu, which was European in style, classic, reserved and controlled. André was also working to make better wines but the research there was being done in an organized, academic manner.

Robert Mondavi Winery was much more American in style, charged with Robert's energy, which drove it forward as fast as it could go. At Mondavi, so many experiments were going on at once and everyone was rushing around — and not in a particularly organized way.

This was not my style. I had been shaped by my time at Beaulieu and by André's way of researching, which was to do one experiment at a time in an orderly fashion. You observed the results, you improved, you learned if it worked or not, and then you improved it a little bit more.

Still, I admired Robert's great energy and his belief in what he was doing. He believed that the answer to raising the quality of wines was in scientific progress, and so he was the first to try many new technologies. Each of the four years I was at his winery he had a new idea. The first year he bought Roto tanks, which are suspended in the air, and which no one else had. He said, "My wines are better because of the Roto tanks."

The next year he bought a centrifuge and he said, "Now my wines are so good because of the centrifuge." Then he bought a filter, and he forgot about the Roto tanks and centrifuge.

He bought a new press. He built a bottling line to protect the wine from oxidation. He even bought French Limousin oak barrels for his white wines, which no one else in Napa Valley was using at the time.

Every Monday we would taste wines, his against the best of the French wines. "Sooner or later we will be able to make wines as good as the French," he would say.

I had ideas but not as many as Robert Mondavi. Many mornings he and I would have breakfast together in his kitchen and talk. I felt we were a good match — I knew he needed my classical training and in return he gave me freedom and responsibility.

Beaulieu's specialty was red wines, not white wines. Robert Mondavi Winery was making both red and white wines, and I continued to work on the problems I had begun to confront at Beaulieu, chiefly to stabilize and improve white wines. I worked with cold fermentation to preserve the natural aromas and flavors from the grapes. I continued to learn more about white wines at Mondavi, but it was a red wine that was my first victory.

It was in this exciting atmosphere that I made my first wine at Mondavi, from the 1969 harvest. We purchased Cabernet Sauvignon grapes from the Stags Leap district, which were harvested at a sugar level of 23.5° brix and .6 grams/100ml of acid. We put them in tank #12 to ferment, 6,000 gallons.

When we tasted this wine, we were surprised at how balanced it was even during its early stages. Only Robert and I knew how exceptional it was, how good it smelled and tasted.

With all of his expenses and still not a lot of money coming in, Robert was short of cash in those first years. One way he could make extra money was to sell the pressed wines as soon as possible to Paul Masson, who had a winery in Saratoga, south of San Francisco. Robert would keep the best wines, the "free-run". This year, however, Paul told Robert he wasn't happy with the samples he was given. "You have to give me some of your best wines," he said.

So Robert gave him 2,000 gallons of the 1969 Cabernet Sauvignon from tank #12, and Paul was happy. My heart was crying when I saw that wine go to Paul Masson. I believed that we had made a perfect wine and we had to let it go.

Several years later in 1972, Robert Balzer, a writer for the *Los Angeles Times*, was collecting samples for a California Cabernet Sauvignon blind tasting that would be sponsored by his newspaper. It was the first such large tasting of Cabernet Sauvignons in California. Balzer chose fifteen judges, including well-known California Cabernet winemakers like Louis Martini, André Tchelistcheff and Joe Heitz.

The 1969 Robert Mondavi Cabernet Sauvignon, the first vintage I made at Robert Mondavi Winery, garnered the highest score — it was declared Number 1, the winner!

Since it was a blind tasting, no one knew whose wine they were tasting. After the Mondavi wine was declared the winner, Joe Heitz asked Mr. Balzer, "Why didn't you put my wine in this tasting?"

Mr. Balzer replied, "I put in your wine; you didn't recognize it." Robert Mondavi didn't recognize his wine either.

For the first time, all of my education and experience had produced results. After so many years of effort I was finally feeling happy — a winner! James Laube, from the Wine Spectator magazine gave the wine 99 points and said it was "possibly the best cab ever made in California."

It was an important victory for Robert Mondavi; many said it "put him on the map." His image and his wines were elevated. His Cabernet ranked now with that of Beaulieu. Some writers pointed out that I had brought Tchelistcheff's classical training to Mondavi's drive and innovation, but it was more than that. I had a preparation that no one else had. I learned from my father that every step in winemaking is important, as is every link in a chain. I was lucky to have been able to work with men who were giants in the world of wine, and I absorbed their knowledge. I put together everything I learned from each of them. So, although I made that wine, it was also my father, the enology degree I received from the University of Zagreb in Croatia, Lee Stewart, Brother Timothy, André Tchelistcheff, my education and my experience that made the best Cabernet in California in 1969.

This victory was only a beginning. I knew now that I, on my own, could make the best wines possible.

One of Robert Mondavi's best qualities was that he always gave credit where credit was due. Twenty-five years after the *Los Angeles Times* tasting, he invited two hundred people — his friends, customers and the media — to dinner and to re-taste the 1969 Cabernet Sauvignon. By then I had been gone from his winery for many years and had already established my own winery, Grgich Hills Cellar. Nonetheless, he invited me to attend and to describe to everyone how I had made the winning 1969 Robert Mondavi Cabernet Sauvignon. He announced, "Mike Grgich made this wine." This was the generous spirit of Robert Mondavi that lifted up everyone around him.

To show how fast things were moving at the Robert Mondavi Winery, when I started in 1968 we crushed five hundred tons of grapes. The next year it had doubled. The next year it doubled again. By the time I left the winery in 1972, Robert Mondavi was crushing five thousand tons!

As production increased and Robert became increasingly successful, I told him, "I need some help. I cannot make all these wines by myself."

"Of course you can," he said. "Miljenko, I know you can handle it."

"No," I said, "I know I cannot." I was proud of my wines. I had to make the best wines. I was a precision winemaker, a perfectionist. I said, "I am not happy if mistakes arise because of the volume and I cannot control it. I want to have total control and perfect wines."

This is how I found Zelma Long in 1970. Mr. Bill Kirby, a

∽ Miljenko "Mike" Grgich

graduate of West Point who had been an assistant to General Douglas MacArthur during the Korean War, was now working in the wine industry, and he told me about Zelma, who was his neighbor in Angwin. Her family had come from Oregon and purchased a hillside vineyard in Napa Valley. Zelma had graduated from Oregon State University and because of her great interest in growing grapes, she went back to school at UC Davis to learn more about viticulture and winemaking. She had just graduated from Davis. I knew that this smart woman would be a good assistant winemaker.

I called her home, and her mother answered the phone. I said, "I would like Zelma to work for Robert Mondavi Winery."

Her mama replied, "Over my dead body." I learned that Zelma's mother had a television station in Oregon and she wanted Zelma to take over the work there. Eventually I was able to talk to Zelma and she accepted my offer to work at Robert Mondavi Winery. When I left Robert, Zelma took over my responsibilities for the next ten years.

I enjoyed working with Zelma. She was well organized and had drive. We spent many hours talking about wine and she understood my viewpoint that a winemaker must have science but must also be an artist, and that there was great value in European traditions as well as modern technology. Also, she understood that a winemaker must possess something intuitive about the work. I soon came to believe that she could do anything, but she complained about the way I worked — that I worked too much and very long hours.

"Mike," she said, "you are not organized. You work sixteen

Zelma Long's first harvest at Robert Mondavi in 1970. I am proud I was able to give Zelma Long her first winery position.

hours a day, all three shifts."

We had three shifts during crush and she was right — I did work all three of them. "Yes, I have to be here," I said. "I have to give orders and ensure that they are accomplished."

Several years after I left Mondavi and Zelma had become the winemaker, I was driving from Chateau Montelena in Calistoga back to my home in Napa at about nine o'clock one evening. It was harvest and I noticed that there were lights in the crushing area at Mondavi winery, so I stopped by. There, on the crushing pad, was Zelma hard at work, giving orders, overseeing the crush. I could not help but smile when I saw her. I remembered what she had told me, but I did not ask her if it was her second or third shift that day.

I was working hard at Mondavi, but I was enjoying living. By this I mean learning, moving forward. Still, when I looked to my future, I wasn't sure it could be at Mondavi. Robert Mondavi had two fine sons, Michael and Tim. Having returned from his military service, Michael worked full-time at the winery. Tim was studying enology at UC Davis when I joined Robert Mondavi Winery and he worked at the winery during his summer vacations. They were both smart, hard-working young men, and I knew they would be in charge one day.

Michael Mondavi was about six feet tall and was always on the move. He was full of energy and passion and was appointed vice president of Robert Mondavi Winery at the age of twenty-two.

When I began working in the winery, Michael was in charge of winemaking and I was responsible for quality control. We were both young and ready to charge! As time went on, Michael became more involved with management. Little by little, I was being given some of Michael's responsibilities in winemaking. We worked closely and had a good working relationship. Often, Michael would take me to the kitchen for breakfast where we would plan our strategy for the day and the future.

Tim Mondavi was a handsome young man and proud of himself. He wore his hair long and was always up for having fun. I enjoyed working with him; he showed his passion for wines and for his girlfriend, a beautiful girl named Dorothy Reed. One day he asked me if I knew of a room or house for rent for her. It happened that the one-room unit at the back of my two-family house at 1212 Edwards Street that I had kept after we moved to Napa was vacant. He inspected the place, liked it and moved Dorothy there for a while. Tim was very responsible at any job he undertook; he would carry it through with satisfaction. I had a feeling that some day he would be a fine winemaker for his father.

Another person I enjoyed working with was Margrit Biever. When I started working for Robert Mondavi Winery, Margrit was in charge of hospitality. She was young and pretty and had come from Europe. She spoke five languages fluently and made friends easily.

My office for quality control was in the tower of the winery. I cherish the many memories I have of that lab in the tower. In those days it was where tastings took place, where we made our analyses and our decisions for the next actions. Robert would always bring Margrit with him for any and all wine tastings. She had a European palate, which he appreciated.

I spent many hours in that lab. To get to it, you had to go through the accounting office on the ground level and then go up the long wooden steps of a circular staircase. Unfortunately, the lab did not have any windows. The only light came from a single light bulb.

One day I was working on an important analysis of the total acid in our red wine lots, with my back to the stairwell, when I heard somebody coming up from the accounting office. I thought it was a good friend coming to visit. When I turned around and looked towards the staircase, I was startled to see a gigantic 200-pound Great Dane staring right at me.

I could not escape because the dog was blocking the top of the staircase. I felt like shouting for help but was afraid that I would provoke the dog into attacking me. I shut my mouth and started praying to St. Anthony to save my life. Since I was standing still — not moving, not talking to the dog — he might have thought that I was not interested in him. He turned around and went down the steps. What a relief when he finally disappeared down the stairs!

Later that day, I was testing bottles of red wine that had been returned from the market as "bad," when one of them slipped from my hand and landed on top of the steps. The bottle started rolling down, one step at a time, until it landed on top of our bookkeeper's big table. There it burst and splashed wine all over the table, which was full of papers and documents. The bookkeeper was surprised, shocked and very mad. I ran downstairs as fast as I could to apologize and clean the table. The bookkeeper ran out in the opposite direction and left the mess with me. That was a bad day for both the bookkeeper and me. I will remember that day for the rest of my life.

Soon Robert Mondavi decided to add a beautiful three-room laboratory upstairs in the brand new warehouse he had just finished building. One room was designed for wine tasting. It was spacious, with a white Formica countertop and many glasses in stock — in short, a very comfortable room.

Another room was to be used for chemical analyses of wine. It was well equipped with all the modern instruments needed for every kind of analysis, including lots of pipettes, a colorimeter, an oxygen meter, a refractometer to measure sugar levels during harvest, and many other instruments.

The third room was to be used for microbiological examinations. There was equipment for sterilizing juice, a microscope, an incubator and Petri dishes.

The lab was state of the art; however, I felt isolated in the bare rooms upstairs. It had no flowers, decorations or pictures, and, like the previous lab room, not one window. The only daylight came in from the sunroof.

Margrit Biever was in charge of the tasting room, which I noticed was decorated with flowers and pictures both inside and outside. One day I went to the tasting room and told Margrit, "The new lab is modern, practical, and scientific. I wish to have some pictures and flowers to make the lab

The new Robert Mondavi Winery.
My lab was at the top of the tower.

She understood what I was trying to say. Margrit offered me the huge flowering plant she had at the entrance of the tasting room. I tried to carry the pot to the lab but she said, "Miljenko, you do not need to carry it. I will have somebody deliver the plant to you." I thanked her, and from that day on my new lab was no longer bare; it had a real, live flower and looked friendly and inviting.

When the Wine Institute informed me that their sanitary and safety inspector was on his way to inspect the Robert Mondavi Winery, we tried to have everything clean and safe. I saw our foreman, Mark, on top of a 20-foot tall tank and told him the inspector was coming. "Do not move if you see the inspector," I said.

Of course, he did not follow instructions. When he noticed the inspector, he stepped on top of a long metal ladder. Suddenly his legs started to shake, the ladder tilted, and he dropped to the floor, close to the inspector! Fortunately he survived without any major injury, although his legs were a little unstable when he got up and started to walk. Thank goodness he was okay, but the inspector did register the accident in his report.

I have many fond memories of the years I worked at Robert Mondavi Winery. Robert truly exerted every effort to make wines as good as the French. He imported from France hundreds of new Limousin oak barrels for aging white wine — Chardonnay and Fumé Blanc (Sauvignon Blanc).

One day Robert's friend, Italian winemaker August Sebastiani, came to visit and to see all the new equipment and barrels. I was walking with the two of them when we came across a huge wall of French barrels, stacked five rows high. August stopped and asked Robert, "What would you do if the barrel in the bottom row starts leaking?"

Robert replied, "I would pump the wine out, plug the leak with 'tooly' and return the wine back to the affected barrel."

August Sebastiani thought that this was not a practical method because the empty barrel at the bottom would be crushed by the weight of the filled barrels above it. He suggested that a better way would be to empty the leaking barrel and fill it up with cement! I laughed. Barrels are made to withstand a great deal of weight and throughout my years of winemaking I have never seen a barrel that was crushed by the weight of barrels above it.

I admired Robert Mondavi, and I learned a great deal from working with him. He was humane and he respected the people who worked for him. He never put himself above anyone and I never saw him put anyone down; he worked as hard as everyone else. He recognized the abilities and the achievements of others. Everyone who worked at his winery was a member of Robert's family. We were all part of the great things that were happening at Robert Mondavi Winery.

From Robert Mondavi I learned that energy and passion, as well as science, are necessary to make good wines. But by now I had my own ideas about winemaking.

One time James Nichelini came to the winery. His family had come from Switzerland and built a small winery in the Chiles Valley of the eastern Napa hills, in 1890, and they kept it running all through Prohibition. Although they sometimes got in trouble with the law, they survived. They are today still a family-owned winery.

James Nichelini brought his 1967 Zinfandel to taste with the Robert Mondavi Zinfandel that I had made. We tasted our two wines side by side. I liked my wine but when I tasted Nichelini's Zinfandel I realized that I liked his better. I wondered why. At Mondavi we had Roto tanks and filters and stainless steel tanks, French barrels, all these modern innovations that Nichelini did not have, and yet, I still preferred his wines.

Something new came to my mind that day: "If I can make wine that people like, that is what counts." How could I do that? Nichelini didn't have our modern equipment, so he didn't process his wines as much as we did. What was the difference? Is there something that no technology or modern equipment can add to a wine? Could it be the soul of the winemaker?

Although I knew that technology was important, I had come to believe that wines must be crafted by an artist winemaker. You have to know the science, but you have to be an artist as well, like a painter or a sculptor whose soul transforms canvas or stone. A winemaker has to have a vision of what the wine should be like, just as a sculptor uncovers a form that is already present in a stone.

Art is commitment, devotion and time. An artist can paint one hundred pictures but not all will be great. He might try and fail many times. Having knowledge alone is not enough: it requires sacrifice to make something unique. You have to achieve more than the ordinary.

After the *Los Angeles Times* tasting of the 1969 Cabernet Sauvignon wines, I received many offers to work at other places. However, I could not see any reason to leave the Mondavi winery, which was the best place to be working, until in early in 1972, when a man named Lee Paschich came to see me at the recommendation of André Tchelistcheff.

Lee owned a winery in Calistoga named Chateau Montelena where he made a little bit of wine, more as a hobby than anything else. He presented me with a very exciting job offer, one that would give me not only a salary but part ownership in a new winery project. I had been in the Napa Valley for almost fifteen years and finally I had a chance to get closer to what I had longed for since I stepped off that Greyhound bus in St. Helena in 1958, or perhaps even earlier, when I got on that train in Zagreb. To take this job would be another step toward my dream: to own something of my own. I spoke to Robert, and he encouraged me. "Go," he said, "and if it doesn't work out, you can always come back."

That is the kind of man Robert Mondavi was. I was lucky to have known and worked for him.

A Napa meeting of the minds. From left to right: Jack Davies, Dick Peterson, Brad Webb (partially obscured), Julius Jacobs, Robert Mondavi, Harry Waugh, Harold Berg from U.C. Davis, Belle Rhodes, Joe Heitz, Lee Stewart, and Brother Timothy.

AT THE FRONT DOOR OF CHATEAU MONTELENA —
FINALLY A LIMITED PARTNER AS WELL AS WINEMAKER.

Chapter 12

Chateau Montelena

Chateau Montelena was one of the ghost wineries of Napa Valley, shut down by Prohibition. It had been, however, the product of grand dreams. The facade of its main building was that of an immense stone castle, complete with two round turrets. But it was only an empty shell, with dirt floors inside, scant electricity and no supply of potable water. The only water source was an underground mineral well. When I visited Chateau Montelena in the early 1970s, it broke my heart to see the neglected state of its vineyards and trees.

Alfred Tubbs had built the winery in the 1880s. He was a San Francisco businessman who had come from New York during the Gold Rush. He made his fortune selling rope, and he decided to spend his fortune building a winery in Napa Valley. Then, as now, the popular joke was: "What does it take to make a small fortune in the wine industry? Start with a large fortune."

Tubbs bought 254 acres at the northern end of Napa Valley, where the western Mayacamas Mountains meet the

Miljenko "Mike" Grgich

Vaca Mountain range from the east, and the Napa River begins. The soil here is good, a mixture from the two mountain ranges, the volcanic east and alluvial west. The climate suits grape-growing, too: it is hot in summers but the nights are cool, and this is an excellent thing for grapes. In the sun, they develop their sugar, but the coolness at night preserves their acidity. You achieve balance.

Tubbs had a great admiration for France. He traveled to France and brought back cuttings from French vineyards, and he wanted his winery to look like the chateaux he had seen in Bordeaux. He hired French architects and craftsmen, and even imported French stone to build a replica of the famous Château Lafite Rothschild winery. And he hired a French winemaker, Jerome Bardot. He named his winery the A.L. Tubbs Winery.

By 1896 it was the seventh largest winery in California, and its wines were in the Paris World's Fair, where California wines won medals. When Tubbs died in 1896, the property passed to his son, William, and then in 1915 to his grandson, Chapin, who renamed it Chateau Montelena, after Mt. St. Helena, which towers over it.

Chapin Tubbs' dreams were destroyed by Prohibition. Chateau Montelena stopped making wine. He managed to keep his property, and he was ready to start making wine when Prohibition ended in 1934, but he was too optimistic about the market for fine wine in America. He went bankrupt.

The family struggled after the bankruptcy, but continued to grow and sell grapes until 1958, when they sold the chateau

Chateau Montelena, Est. 1882

to a couple by the name of Yort and Jeanie Frank, who wanted to use it as a home for their retirement. They decided that their castle needed a moat, and they began to dig one. Eventually they gave up on this project and left it as a lake. They named it Jade Lake and built pagodas on small islands in the lake to remind Mr. Frank of his own homeland, China. Ten years later, they decided to sell the property.

Leland and Helen Paschich lived in San Francisco where they had a business, Shades, Inc., which made bamboo wood window coverings designed by Helen. Lee, a wine hobbyist, was looking for a lab and cellar. In 1968 they bought Chateau Montelena from the Franks and moved Shades, Inc. to a new building close to the old winery. Other than some home winemaking from the grapes that had been grown there, wine had not been made at Chateau Montelena for more that 50 years.

I met Lee Paschich at the Robert Mondavi Winery during the 1971 harvest when he delivered five wooden bins full of Chardonnay grapes from his Calistoga vineyard on Pickett Road. Lee asked that his grapes be crushed right away but the winery had just finished its daily crush when he arrived. We could not start crushing again just for five bins, so we decided to store his grapes overnight and crush them the next day. We put the bins next to stainless steel tanks that had a coat of ice. This ice would protect the grapes from oxidation.

The next morning, when I came into the winery and turned on the light, I noticed something moving slightly on the floor of the walkway. As I came closer, it curled up into a coil. It was a rattlesnake! I realized it had probably ridden into the winery with Lee Paschich's Chardonnay grapes. Calistoga was well known for having many rattlesnakes.

Quickly I grabbed a wooden bung starter, the mallet we use to remove the stopper (or bung) from a barrel. I walked very carefully towards the snake until I was close enough to hit it on the head. It died instantly. I buried it under a tree and then went on with my daily work. I was not likely to forget my first meeting with Lee Paschich!

About six months later, in the spring of 1972, he called to ask if he could come to see me. He was smiling and happy when he arrived at the Robert Mondavi Winery. We joked about the rattlesnake he had accidentally brought to the winery. Then he became serious.

"Mike," he said, "I have brought in two gentlemen from Southern California to be partners at Chateau Montelena. They would like to restart winemaking at the chateau but they need a winemaker. Would you talk to them?"

The next day I went to the offices of Shades, Inc. in Calistoga, where I met with Lee and James Barrett, a lawyer who was one of the new general partners. The other partner was Ernie Hahn, a real estate developer. The conversation was friendly but straight to the point: they asked me about my experience at Beaulieu Vineyard making Cabernet Sauvignon with André Tchelistcheff.

Jim Barrett, I learned, was interested in purchasing Chateau Montelena with the goal of making a Cabernet

Sauvignon that would be as good as the best wines of Bordeaux. Ultimately, he wanted to make a wine that rivaled the great wine from Château Lafite. To keep the quality high, he said, the winery would be small. Hearing "small" was music to my ears! Crushing five thousand tons of grapes at Robert Mondavi Winery, as we were currently doing, did not give me enough time to pay attention to details. I liked the idea of joining a "small-size" winery.

Jim Barrett not only offered me a job with a salary, but he added in a one percent per year ownership of Chateau Montelena. This interested me very much.

Lee Paschich took me on a tour around Chateau Montelena. Outside the building was an old wooden press, for decoration, but inside all I saw were several empty barrels. Lee told me he would remove the empty barrels soon. In 1968 he made some Cabernet Sauvignon and was now selling it for $1 a bottle. I was amused to see Jade Lake, a beautiful but untended lake surrounded by weeping willows. In this small lake were several tiny islands with Chinese gazebos on them connected by red zigzag bridges, and a dilapidated Chinese junk on the shore. I liked it and thought that perhaps I would fish here some day.

I also saw that I had a lot of work ahead of me if we were going to create a winery in this empty shell and be ready to make wine by September. I would have to hire people, buy grapes and purchase *foudre* barrels, a crusher, a hopper, pumps and everything else required to be ready for the crush. We would have to pull out the old grapes and plant Cabernet Sauvignon.

Still, I was very excited by the offer to be the winemaker and limited partner. For me it was a golden opportunity. I had always been working under somebody else but now I would be on my own, in charge of the operation of the winery. The owners would entrust me with this responsibility because they were off site, based in Los Angeles. I would be independent but I would also have to have good judgment to make the right decisions at the right time if I were going to make Chateau Montelena a successful winery under my leadership.

And I would also have one percent ownership. My dream to be the winemaker and own part of a winery would become a reality. Here was another miracle!

I told Jim Barrett that I first had to talk to Robert Mondavi because by then the house of Mondavi and the house of Grgich were almost like one. The next day I went to Robert and said, "Bob, I would like to take a one-month leave of absence. Some people are starting a new winery and they want me to be the winemaker. They are willing to give me part of the ownership."

Robert replied, "Mike, if that is true it is a big improvement over what you have here. I have two sons and a daughter. I cannot give you a partnership. I cannot match that offer. Take the month off and good luck. If it doesn't work out, you will always be welcome here."

Two weeks later, after further talks with Barrett and Paschich, I was back in Robert's office. "Bob, these people want me to go ahead," I said. "They look to be nice people and serious."

≪ Miljenko "Mike" Grgich

"Mike, just be sure everything is clear, on paper and signed — especially regarding the percentage of ownership of Chateau Montelena," he advised. "Get a clean-cut agreement, and get it in writing. Otherwise don't do it."

On May 8, 1972, I started my new job at Chateau Montelena as a limited partner with a five-year contract. I was there at 8 a.m. Shortly after, Helen Paschich walked into the office and brought me paper, a pencil, a pen and a ruler to start the design of Chateau Montelena Winery. She wished me good luck. Lee Paschich followed and he reminded me that Mr. Barrett needed a five-year budget. I was going to have plenty of work on my first day!

First I devised a budget: I drew a line down a sheet of paper dividing it in half. On one side of the sheet I put all the expenses: equipment, electricity, the cost of the grapes and labor. The other side, where the profit should be, was blank. There would be no income for at least five years if the owners were determined to make only Cabernet Sauvignon. When I presented the proposed budget to the new owners of Chateau Montelena, they were horrified.

"What is this?" they asked me. "How can it be that we won't make any profit for five years?"

"Great wine cannot be made in a hurry," I explained. "It is a process and a good winemaker must give wine time to mature." I told them that after we replanted the vineyards, it would be four years before the grapes could produce wines. Jim Barrett wanted to make only Cabernet Sauvignon as good as Château Lafite in Bordeaux. In order to make high quality

Cabernet it had to be aged in barrels for several years before it could be released and sold. Therefore, it would take at least five years for the 1972 vintage to be ready for the market, which meant that during this time we would only incur expenses and have no income.

Jim Barrett was surprised at this. He said, "No way. This budget will make us broke. Is there any other way to go so that we can have some income as soon as possible?" With all that they had invested, he said, they needed to make money right away.

"Well, then," I said, "we should make a white wine because it does not have to age as long as red wine."

Making white and red wines, I explained, was the best way to obtain a cash flow sooner because the whites would provide profits for five years until the Cabernet Sauvignon could be put on the market.

I went back to my desk and drew up a proposal that would provide a cash flow as soon as possible. I suggested starting off by making some white wines, like Riesling, that we could crush in September and put on the market in spring 1973. The second wine to make would be Chardonnay. It would take a little longer because Chardonnay would have to age in oak barrels before it would be ready to be bottled, but we could sell it in two years. We could crush Chardonnay in September 1972 and start selling in 1974 or 1975. We could also start making Cabernet Sauvignon and Zinfandel in 1972 with purchased grapes.

I presented the alternative budget to Jim Barrett when he came back from Los Angeles. He thought that it looked better, especially because I proposed to make a Cabernet Sauvignon and a Zinfandel from the 1972 vintage.

One thing I insisted on, however, was that I had to buy the best grapes I could find. I explained that many wineries bought grapes, including Robert Mondavi Winery. Only old established wineries like Beaulieu Vineyard were able to grow their own.

"Mike, this budget looks reasonable," Jim Barrett said. "Go ahead."

Had I not convinced the new owners that whites would bring in their much-needed cash flow, Chateau Montelena would never have made white wines, especially Chardonnay. But none of us could have imagined at this point what the decision to make Chardonnay would mean for all of us in only a few years.

With the budget and my plan approved, now I could concentrate on creating a working winery. Harvest was four months away and I needed to be ready to receive the grapes. I was a vintner, a winemaker, and never before had I had the need to design a winery. I called an engineer who had worked for Robert Mondavi and explained my predicament. "Could you give me some advice?" I asked.

He told me that designing a winery was easy. First, I had to measure the floor area of the winery, and then convert the numbers from feet to inches or centimeters so I could make models for the equipment, the tanks, hopper, crusher, press and barrels. He told me to call him if I had any problems.

I carefully followed his advice and created a floor plan. I

was on my way. Now I had only to clean the interior of the old chateau, reconnect electricity and running water, and find the equipment. Did I sweat? Yes, of course, but I did all this work with excitement.

Chateau Montelena had a vineyard behind the winery of about one hundred and sixteen acres, which was planted with several grape varieties: white Chasselas, red Alicante Bouschet and Carignan, plus 10 acres of Zinfandel that Lee had just planted.

The grapes, except for the Zinfandel, were sold to other wineries because they were not on par with the quality envisioned by both Jim Barrett and myself. We decided, therefore, to replace the Chasselas, Alicante Bouschet and Carignan vines with premium grapes. In 1972, we pulled out the old vines and bought phylloxera-resistant St. George rootstock budded with high-quality Cabernet Sauvignon from the vineyard of Wallace Johnson in Alexander Valley. John Rolleri, an expert vineyard manager, supervised the replanting of the vineyards.

Meanwhile, I was equipping the cellar. First I bought a thirty-year-old used crusher from Inglenook that was still functioning. We could use it for a few years until we could afford to buy a new crusher. Next I ordered a hopper and hoist from John Kalua, and stainless steel jacketed tanks from a factory in Santa Rosa. I ordered the press from Modesto and bought wooden upright tanks and barrels from Sterling Vineyards in Calistoga.

I had never realized the amount of responsibilities an

∽ Miljenko "Mike" Grgich

independent winemaker has. It was particularly difficult to buy quality grapes. In those days there were not many top quality grapes available, so one had to beg and practically kneel to high-end grape growers so they would sell to you. Since the demand was more than the supply, the price per ton of grapes was going up every year.

The grapes for the Chateau Montelena vintage 1972 came from contracts made with John Hanna to buy Riesling and Chardonnay from his Orchard Avenue vineyards in Napa Valley. We bought Chardonnay and Cabernet Sauvignon from Lee Paschich that he'd grown on his Pickett Road ranch in Calistoga, and I bought Chardonnay grapes from Redwood Ranch in Alexander Valley in Sonoma.

Before the crush, I also had to organize a cellar crew. It included Roam Steineke, who was Ernie Hahn's son-in-law, Jim Barrett's son Bo Barrett, and Ron Sculatti, who lived in nearby St. Helena.

When all the preparations were done, I was finally able to envision the crush of 1972. I set the beginning of September as the date for our first crush. Everything and everyone was ready — the equipment was clean and sterilized, and ready to go. On the appointed day, we gathered our friends and relatives, employees and growers together, and at 10 a.m. John Hanna delivered a gondola filled with his Chardonnay grapes.

Jim Barrett's brother, Father Vincent Barrett, was a priest who was visiting us from the Los Angeles diocese. Following an old European tradition, Father Vincent blessed the grapes as well as all those present, and he prayed for a successful and

Our first Blessing of the Grapes on September 1, 1972. To my right are partners Jim Barrett and Lee Paschich, and Jim's brother Father Vincent Barrett.

safe harvest. After the prayers, he sprinkled Holy Water on the grapes and on us.

The hoist lifted the gondola, tipped it over and the grapes fell into the new hopper. The screw conveyor rotated and started moving grapes to the crusher. It was a happy beginning of a new life for Chateau Montelena and we celebrated with good food and toasted with fine wine. I started to sing my favorite American song, "You Are My Sunshine."

Our hopes to make a profit rested with the white wine grapes, which are harvested earlier than the red. I knew I had to craft a better wine than I had ever made before. I had to take the best lessons I had learned in each place I had worked and combine them to make my own style of wine. I used all of my knowledge and experience, what I had absorbed from my father, from the professors in Zagreb, from Lee Stewart, Brother Timothy, André Tchelistcheff and Robert Mondavi. With all the education and experience I received, I felt very confident starting the first harvest at Chateau Montelena.

In 1972, our first year, we were prepared to encounter problems with the winery and equipment, but we could not predict the weather. During the peak of crush there would be twelve consecutive days of non-stop rain, a disaster for grapes. Fortunately, the more sensitive Johannisberg Riesling and Chardonnay had been picked before the rain, but the Cabernet Sauvignon grapes were still hanging in the vineyard. I checked the sugar and acid every day. On the sixth day, wild mold appeared on the clusters of Cabernet. It was time to harvest them but the rain was still strong and steady. After twelve days of continuous rain, the sun finally appeared and the crew started to pick Cabernet in Calistoga and in Sonoma.

As a result of this weather, the 1972 Cabernet Sauvignon grapes did not have the quality we desired, and so we decided to label and sell it under another name, Silverado Cellars. Jim Barrett's dream of producing a red wine as good as Chateau Lafite from the first vintage did not materialize, but this was another important lesson for new vintners: You can plan and hope and dream but in the end, it's Mother Nature who decides what kind of wine you are going to make.

On the other hand, the 1972 Chateau Montelena white wines turned out to be a huge success. The Johannisberg Riesling was the first wine we put on the market. To make this wine, I recalled and applied everything I had learned from my teachers and mentors. Lee Stewart's Johannisberg Riesling had been admired, but the Beaulieu Riesling was less popular. The Beaulieu Riesling was quite dry and not very food-friendly, and wine is meant to be enjoyed with food. At Robert Mondavi, the Johannisberg Riesling had one percent residual sugar, which people liked; it sold much better than the Beaulieu Riesling. I made the Chateau Montelena Riesling to be pleasant and left two percent sugar by stopping fermentation. We called it "Late Harvest," a term used by Germans to signify a slightly sweet wine.

The price of the 1972 Johannisberg Riesling was $5.50 retail for a 750 ml bottle. It caught the attention of critics perhaps because its touch of sweetness appealed to the American taste. At a tasting organized by the *Los Angeles Times*,

∽ Miljenko "Mike" Grgich

it won "California's Golden Eagle Award" as one of the ten best California Rieslings. In October 1975 wine critic Robert Finigan wrote of the 1974 Johannisberg Riesling, "Intriguing flavors combine with an elegant style and long finish to produce what I consider one of the finest California Rieslings currently obtainable."

Chateau Montelena was on its way to success!

Unlike the Riesling, the 1972 Chardonnay had a rocky start. We made eight hundred cases, and because it was aged in new French oak barrels, I decided I would leave it in the bottles longer so its flavors would not be dominated by oak; eight months would give it a balance of both grape and oak aromas.

When we bottled this wine, calamity struck. I had all of the essential equipment in place, but what I did not yet have was a vacuum attachment for the corker. This attachment removes the oxygen in the neck of the wine bottle so the cork goes into an oxygen-free space. Without this vacuum attachment the wine might oxidize; however, many wineries bottled without it and nothing went wrong.

We had ordered the vacuum attachment but the mechanic who was supposed to install it got sick and was unable to finish the job before we bottled the 1972 Chardonnay. After bottling, I watched the bottles to see if everything was all right. It was approximately one month later that I noticed that the color of the wine started to change into brownish pink hues. I was shocked and immediately called Jim Barrett so he could see the color and taste the wine with me. We both concluded that the taste of the wine was perfect but the color had changed.

I continued to watch the color for the next two months. Just when I was feeling great despair, the wine began to clear up. I noticed that the golden color was slowly beginning to return. Again I called Jim Barrett to show him. The color was now golden, and the taste was even better than the first time we tasted it — one more miracle for me.

The 1972 Chateau Montelena wines, the first vintage I crafted, were doing well with the new tasting groups that started to become fashionable in the early 1970s. Many Americans became acquainted with good wine through clubs such as the Berkeley Wine and Food Society or the many chapters of *Les Amis du Vin*. The members often used a scoring system designed by professors at UC Davis, and brought a systematic approach to wine tasting. It was not good enough to say that you liked this wine or not; now you had to explain why and describe the flavors and aromas you experienced.

The most important society was the San Francisco Vintners Club, which held its first tasting on June 21, 1973. This elite group of wine professionals and amateurs met every Thursday afternoon at 4:30 for a blind tasting of an average of twelve wines of a specific category such as Zinfandel or Sauternes. The Chateau Montelena 1972 Johannisberg Riesling was part of a tasting on June 16, 1974 and comments from it noted the wine's "small but elegant nose." The 1972 Chateau Montelena Chardonnay took center stage the following month and was described as having an "excellent Chardonnay nose."

On October 27, 1974, the *San Diego Grapevine* newspaper reported that ten Chardonnays had been compared by the

"Feisty Friends of the Vine" at their meeting at Zolezzi's Restaurant. The 1972 Chateau Montelena Chardonnay took first place when they ranked the wines.

Later that year, they blind-tasted two Chardonnays, the 1972 Chateau Montelena and one of the most famous white Burgundies from France, Bâtard-Montrachet, also from the 1972 vintage. Once again, the Chateau Montelena was chosen, by three out of four judges, to take first place. At the time, the 1972 Bâtard-Montrachet cost $17.50 a bottle, while the 1972 Chateau Montelena was selling for $6.

The hard work and long hours I put in to re-establish Chateau Montelena as a working winery after 50 years of being abandoned had paid off with the triumph of the 1972 Chardonnay. I felt that I was doing something right. It was only my first vintage and it was already winning over the best French wines. I would continue working even harder to craft the perfect wine. Robert Mondavi's dream that we, in Napa Valley, can make as good wine as the French was starting to be fulfilled.

The principals of Chateau Montelena, Jim Barrett, Ernie Hahn and Lee Paschich, were elated. They could see that the winery had a bright future. Their investment was safe and it would pay off. They sent me for a vacation to Hawaii and as an added bonus Ernie Hahn gave me eight hundred shares of his company stocks. It had a face value of only three cents a share at the time but by 1977 I would be able to sell the shares back to Jim Barrett for $45,000.

When I returned from Hawaii, it was time to start thinking

about the 1973 wines. This second year we had had time to become better equipped and we were ready to produce an even better Chardonnay. The cellar at Chateau Montelena now had a laboratory. We had seven American and Yugoslavian oak tanks, with about a 2,000-gallon capacity each. We had eleven stainless steel jacketed fermenters, with about a 3,500-gallon capacity each. We had one stainless steel bladder press; one stainless steel hopper to receive the grapes; one hoist to unload the grapes from the gondolas on the trucks; one crusher, made in Healdsburg, with a capacity to crush ten tons an hour; and one hundred new French oak barrels, from Limousin oak, with a capacity of sixty gallons each.

We used oak barrels for two reasons. First, in the barrel the wine receives a small amount of oxygen through the pores of the oak and the bunghole during the topping off of the wine. This allows the wine to breathe and encourages a chemical reaction called polymerization, which combines tannin molecules into longer chains and gives the wine a smoother texture. Secondly, the oak staves leach wood extracts into wine; these extracts enrich the body, flavor, aromas and color. The wine looks, smells and tastes better. But then, as now, my goal was to create balance in wine. I did not want oak to dominate the flavors of the grapes. Timing is the secret to achieving balance between oak and wine, with about eight months being the answer in this case.

We had contracts to buy Chardonnay grapes from Lee Paschich in Calistoga and from Napa growers John Hanna and his son Bill. In 1973 we bought four tons at a cost of $725 a ton. I also bought Chardonnay grapes from Belle Terre Vineyards

◌ Miljenko "Mike" Grgich

in Alexander Valley. Harry Dick and his son Ron owned these five-year old vineyards. Harry was originally from France and cared for his vines like they were his children. I also contracted to buy Chardonnay grapes from Charles and Helen Bacigalupi in the Russian River region of Sonoma County.

My custom was to go out to the vineyards to see pruning early in the spring, and again in April to see the beginning of "bud break" when the buds open. At the end of May and beginning of June, I checked on the flowering and setting of the berries. By July, I would be visiting the grapes every week. In the second half of July, I began to check the sugar level of the grapes with a refractometer in the vineyard. I would take samples back to the lab to check the acid and pH levels, and recheck the sugar. In the middle of August, I visited the vines every two or three days, checking and rechecking the health, color and especially the taste and aroma of the grapes. As a result, I got to know the vines very well, and I would taste so many berries that sometimes I couldn't eat lunch or dinner.

In the vineyard I would pick anywhere from two hundred to five hundred berries from different positions on the clusters, different clusters on the vines, and from different areas in the vineyards in order to obtain a representative sample. I would crush the berries in a small plastic dish or bag and place a few drops of grape juice on the refractometer to read the Brix (level of sugar) in the juice. I would recheck the results back in the lab.

When the sugar reached 21° Brix, the staff began to get ready for crush. They washed, sterilized and greased the machines. They made sure that there was room for all the fruit that would be arriving. We constantly checked and rechecked everything. We held meetings to be sure everyone was ready. A week before harvest, we met daily to be sure that everybody knew what to do and how to do their assigned responsibility.

The 1973 grapes were healthy with no mold or mildew. When the grapes reached about $22.5°$ — $23.5°$ Brix and all the elements had reached a balance of sugar, acid, pH, character and varietal color, they were ready to pick. The grapes were delivered: one ton from Lee Paschich, four tons from John and Bill Hanna, 20 tons from Belle Terre Vineyards in Alexander Valley, and 14 tons from Charles and Helen Bacigalupi.

The first to arrive were John Hanna's grapes, pulled in by Gary Morisoli and his girlfriend, Melody, who stayed to attend the Blessing of the Grapes.

The excitement and celebration of the crush began. On September 6, 1973, our growers, friends, and family joined proprietors Jim Barrett, Ernie Hahn and Lee Paschich, the three cellar workers, Roam Steineke, Bo Barrett and Ron Sculatti, and myself, the winemaker, to receive and see the first load of grapes crushed. For the second year, Father Vincent Barrett came from Los Angeles to bless the grapes. After the Blessing, a hoist lifted the gondola off the truck bed and tipped the contents into the hopper.

The harvest had begun at dawn, when the grapes were cool, and continued throughout the day. Workers picked the grapes into plastic tubs that held about 40 pounds each.

◆ Miljenko "Mike" Grgich

These were dumped into gondolas that held about four tons of grapes. Tractors pulled the gondolas between the vine rows, and when the gondolas were full, they were taken immediately to the winery. There they were hoisted up and the grapes were dumped into the hopper. A conveyor moved the grapes into the crusher.

The crusher removed the berries from the stems, and pumped them to the press. The stems were later spread as mulch in the vineyards. From the crusher, the berries were then gently pressed and the juice pumped into stainless steel tanks, where it was left to settle for two to three days at a cool temperature of 45-50 degrees Fahrenheit. After it had settled, the clear juice was moved to an empty tank and analyzed for its levels of acid and SO_2, sulfur dioxide. Corrections were made, if necessary, to the acid and SO_2, and yeast was added to start fermentation. We used French White yeast, developed by the Pasteur Institute in Paris. We kept the temperature at 45-50 degrees throughout fermentation, about a month and a half.

When fermentation was completed, the wine was then racked off the spent yeast cells and sediment into another tank, and the temperature was lowered to 30 degrees Fahrenheit for cold stabilization. Later, heat stabilization and clarity was achieved by fining the wine with the necessary amount of bentonite, a type of clay, which causes suspended soluble substances to precipitate. It stayed in these tanks for three weeks.

Then the wine was filtered and moved to the oak barrels for maturing. These barrels had already been used for eight months for the 1972 Chardonnay, which meant that the barrels were seasoned and the rough tannins from the wood removed. This gave the 1973 Chardonnay more elegance and softness. We aged it in oak barrels for eight months in the cellar where the temperature was a constant 50-60 degrees. We used lab analyses to make sure the wine was balanced, and topped it off every two weeks to replace any wine lost to evaporation.

After eight months in barrels, the 1973 Chardonnay was moved out of barrels into stainless steel tanks and a master blend of the wine was made from all of the barrels. We filtered the blend using the Millipore filters that had been developed at Beaulieu for microbiological stability, and bottled it in December 1974. Bottling went smoothly this time, since the vacuum attachment on the corker was now properly installed and was able to prevent any oxidation. The 1973 Chardonnay was a perfect wine from the beginning, and it never turned pink or brown. The bottles were stored at 50-60 degrees for 10 months.

This is the blending of science and the art of winemaking, and each step is important. It is like a chain, where each link is just as important as the next. This last stage, bottle aging, allows the wine to harmonize all of its elements — grapes, oak and yeast — to become more interesting and complex and to develop a beautiful bouquet. Aging, for wine, is a good thing!

I tasted the 1973 Chardonnay while it was still in the barrel, and the aroma and flavors were exciting and well balanced. When the English wine expert Harry Waugh unexpectedly visited Chateau Montelena on May 4, 1974, I climbed up on

Pulling barrel samples for Harry Waugh with a "wine thief."

top of the barrels with a special pipette, called a wine thief, to get a sample for him to taste.

"Mike," Harry said, "I have never had such a good Chardonnay, not even in Paris."

I almost fell off the barrels.

The owners of Chateau Montelena organized a tasting on May 27 and 28, 1975 in San Diego. Both my 1972 and 1973 Chardonnay would be blind-tasted with three of the most famous white Burgundies: Meursault-Jadot, Puligny-Montrachet and Bâtard-Montrachet, Drouhin.

And the results? On May 27, in first place was the 1972 Chateau Montelena Chardonnay, and in second place was the 1973 Chateau Montelena. The Bâtard-Montrachet was third, Meursault-Jadot, fourth and the Puligny-Montrachet was fifth.

At a second blind tasting the next day, the 1973 Chateau Montelena won first place. Number two was Meursault-Jadot. The 1972 Chateau Montelena was in third place; fourth place was Bâtard-Montrachet; and fifth place was Puligny-Montrachet.

I had won two victories in two days. I felt like I was floating in the air. After the San Diego tasting, Ernie Hahn said, "Come on, Mike, I am going to take you to New York City."

He flew Jim Barrett and me to New York aboard his own private plane that was piloted by his son. We ate and drank for two days at "The Windows on the World," the restaurant on the 107th floor of the World Trade Center overlooking "The City That Never Sleeps". This was quite an exciting experience

∽ Miljenko "Mike" Grgich

for me, who still carried memories of not having enough food, of worrying about every penny that I had to spend.

I learned that weekend that Ernie Hahn, who grew up in the Depression, had been unable to attend college, and, like me, had hardly any capital when he began his business. His years of hard work paid off for him, because eventually when he decided to sell his company, called Hahn Co., a Canadian conglomerate bought it in 1980 for $270 million. He was a good and philanthropic human being who liked to enjoy the profits of his hard work.

The San Diego victories had reassured me that I could craft a wine that perhaps would be recognized as one of the best in the world. I had put my body and soul into making those first white wines at Chateau Montelena, but when I think back to those days, one special memory stands out for me.

One day, my little daughter Violet came with me to Chateau Montelena and we walked along Jade Lake, a beautiful, peaceful place that reminded me of the lake back in my village of Desne, in Croatia. Looking across the lake, Violet saw a something glittering in the water not far from the shore. She stepped into the shallow water and came back with a tiny brass bell on a yellow string, caught in a small branch. We were puzzled as to how it had gotten there. Whose bell was it?

I thought of the bell tower of St. George Church in Desne, which had deep meaning for me. Here was my daughter, born in America, with two parents who had such strong ties to the old country that had been taken away from us by Communists, a place she might never be able to see. A bell on a string in a lake — the symbolism seemed like a little miracle to me.

Violet carried her "treasure" with her everywhere, and a couple years later, when she was about 11, we found ourselves in Big Sur delivering wine to an inn where we were going to have dinner and spend the weekend. When we got out of the car, Violet noticed that the porch of the inn was lined with dozens of the very same bell that she had found at Jade Lake years before. After the proprietor greeted us, Violet showed him her bell and, looking surprised, he asked, "Where did you find that?"

When she told him, he explained: "I travel throughout the world and when I find a special place, I hide one of these bells in the hope that a very special person will someday find it. I tied that bell to a tree on Jade Lake, and now that bell has brought us together. I can truly say that this is a miracle!"

I believe that God was with me during this time, as He had been so many times before. But I didn't know then that the next miracle in store for me was just ahead, in 1976.

ENJOYING A BEAUTIFUL DAY ROWING ON
JADE LAKE WITH VIOLET AND TATJANA.

May 24, 1976 — Judges at the Hotel InterContinental in Paris trying the first wines of the tasting. Steven Spurrier is front right. Patricia Gallagher sits to his right.

Chapter 13

The Judgment of Paris

The news came to Chateau Montelena in a telegram with one sentence: "We won in Paris."

Back in Calistoga, I didn't know what it meant. What had we won? Then, I got a telephone call from *The New York Times*. They wanted to talk to me. Why? I thought I must have done something bad to be getting a call from *The New York Times*.

"What did I do wrong?" I asked.

"Nothing," was the reply from the caller at the other end of the line. "We want to interview you about the 1973 Chardonnay that won the Paris tasting."

Three *Times* reporters flew from New York City to California and came up to Calistoga to interview me. Had they ever come to Calistoga to cover a story before? I didn't think so.

From these reporters, I learned the details of a blind tasting that had taken place at the InterContinental Hotel in Paris on May 24, 1976. The 1973 Chardonnay, our second vintage at Chateau Montelena, had been entered into this tasting along with other California wines, all to be judged alongside the most famous of the French wines. Without knowing which were French wines and which were California wines, French judges tasted and gave points to each wine, When the numbers were added up, my Chardonnay received the most points; judged against the great white wines of Burgundy, it had been named the best. Yes. The 1973 Chardonnay I crafted for Chateau Montelena scored 132 points — more points than any California or French Chardonnay included in the blind tasting! When I finally fully understood this, I was filled with such joy and happiness, I began to sing in Croatian. I, the serious guy in the winery, began to dance.

And there was more good news for California: the Cabernet Sauvignon of Stag's Leap Wine Cellars in the Napa Valley had come out with the highest points for the red wines.

In the article that soon came out in *The New York Times*, Frank J. Prial wrote, "The fact is that the best American vineyards and wineries can produce extraordinary wines."

I felt reborn. All the long years of learning and working, learning more and working harder, all the days and nights I spent in vineyards, labs and cellars had borne the sweetest fruit, the best harvest of my life! Was it all luck that I had made such a wine and this wine had gone to Paris and won?

I have an answer for this. As the philosopher says, "When preparation meets opportunity — that is luck."

There have been many articles written about the Paris tasting. George Taber, now my friend, was the only journalist present at the event, and in his book *The Judgment of Paris* he gives a finely detailed account of how the tasting came to be and how it changed the world of wine.

I, who was not there and did not even know the tasting was taking place, can only tell the story as I heard it.

An Englishman by the name of Steven Spurrier owned a wine shop in Paris called Caves de la Madeleine, as well as the Académie du Vin, a wine school offering six-week courses. He and his American associate, Patricia Gallagher, knew and followed the progress that was being made in winemaking in California. They had tasted some excellent wines from America.

They came up with the idea of having a blind tasting of French wines versus the little-known California wines in 1976, to salute America's bicentennial and to publicize his wine shop. They would have French judges taste the finest French white wines of Burgundy and red wines of Bordeaux alongside California wines. I do not think anyone really expected the outcome that actually happened.

Spurrier and Gallagher began collecting the American wines. Robert Finigan, a wine journalist, had tasted my Chateau Montelena 1972 Chardonnay, and he suggested to Steven Spurrier that the next time he was in Napa Valley he should visit Mike Grgich and taste his Chardonnay. Spurrier came to the Napa Valley with his wife, Bella, for the first time early in 1976. Although I did not meet them then, they decided to put my Chardonnay in the tasting. Perhaps they were also aware of the results of the San Diego Tasting of May 27 and 28, 1975 — when both of my Chardonnays had won over three renowned white Burgundies.

❧ Miljenko "Mike" Grgich

Once the California wines had been chosen, the big problem was how to get them to Paris in time for the tasting, set for May 24.

Joanne Dickenson DePuy owned a travel agency in Napa that organized wine tours to France. She had scheduled a tour from Champagne to Bordeaux that would be led by André Tchelistcheff. This was to take place in May 1976. Many Napa Valley vintners signed up for the tour, among them Jim Barrett, the co-owner of Chateau Montelena.

Patricia Gallagher asked Joanne to help her bring the California wines to Paris in the most economical way. When I met Joanne some time later, she told me about the hassle she had to go through to bring the California wines to Paris, especially figuring out how to get twenty-six bottles through customs. She had thought that it would be easy since she had a group going to France. She did not realize until they were checking in that only one bottle of wine was allowed for each passenger. She hastily unpacked the wines she had in a box and gave one bottle to each member of her group. If Joanne had not agreed to serve as a "wine courier" and had not had such presence of mind during check-in for the flight to Paris, the California wines would never have arrived in time for the Paris tasting.

The event was held at the InterContinental Hotel in Paris. George M. Taber, who was then the American correspondent for *Time* Magazine in Paris, attended the tasting. He was the only journalist present because all the other journalists, who were French, expected the French to win, of course, so where was the news in that? Many years later, during a visit to my

A Glass Full of Miracles

home in Calistoga, George told me that since he was the only reporter present he was given a list of the order of the wines being tasted and was allowed to walk around the room and hear the comments of the judges first-hand. Since he spoke French, he could understand everything they were saying. He undoubtedly got the scoop of a lifetime!

The California white wines included in the Paris tasting were Chardonnays from:

- Chalone Vineyards, 1974
- Chateau Montelena, 1973
- David Bruce Winery, 1973
- Freemark Abbey Winery, 1972
- Spring Mountain Vineyard, 1973
- Veedercrest Vineyards, 1972

The French white wines were legendary Chardonnays from Burgundy:*

- Bâtard-Montrachet, (Ramonet-Prudhon), 1973
- Beaune Clos des Mouches, (Joseph Drouhin), 1973
- Meursault Charmes (Roulot), 1973
- Puligny-Montrachet "Les Pucelles," (Domaine Leflaive), 1972

---

*The names in parentheses are the owners of the Burgundy estates where the wines were produced, except for Joseph Drouhin, a wine-shipping firm, *négociant*, who purchased wine from the Clos de Mouches vineyards, blended and bottled it.

For the red wines, the Cabernet Sauvignons from California were:

- Clos du Val Winery, 1972
- Freemark Abbey Winery, 1969
- Heitz Cellars Martha's Vineyard, 1970
- Mayacamas Vineyards, 1971
- Ridge Vineyards Monte Bello, 1971
- Stag's Leap Wine Cellars, 1973

From the Bordeaux region of France, famous for centuries for its Cabernet Sauvignon wines, the wines were:

- Château Haut-Brion, 1970
- Château Léoville-Las-Cases, 1971
- Château Montrose, 1970
- Château Mouton Rothschild, 1970

The judges were all famous too. They included:

- Pierre Bréjoux, Inspector General of the Appellation d'Origine Contrôlée Board, which controlled the production of the top French wines
- Michel Dovaz, teacher of wine courses at the Académie du Vin
- Claude DuBois-Millot, Sales Director of Gault Millau, a publisher of a leading French wine and food magazine and guide

The New York Times

WEDNESDAY JUNE 9, 1976

WINE TALK
By FRANK J. PRIAL

CALIFORNIA LABELS OUTDO FRENCH IN BLIND TEST

"Several California white wines triumphed over some of the best Burgundy has to offer in a blind tasting in Paris recently. More startling: The judges were French…"

"The fact is that the best American vineyards and wineries can produce extraordinary wines. Admittedly the wines in this tasting are from the premium wineries, are in extremely short supply and cost a great deal of money—anywhere from $6 to $20 a bottle. But the same is true of the Burgundies…"

"Miljenko 'Mike' Grgich, the winemaker at Chateau Montelena, said he made 1,800 cases of the 1973 Chardonnay; all of which has been sold. The wine was fermented extremely slowly and spent six months in French oak barrels before bottling…"

Miljenko "Mike" Grgich at Chateau Montelena

JUNE 7, 1976

TIME

Judgement of Paris

Americans abroad have been boasting for years about California wines, only to be greeted in most cases by polite disbelief—or worse. Among the few fervent and respected admirers of *le vin de Californie* in France is a transplanted Englishman, Steven Spurrier, 34, who owns the Cave de la Madeleine wine shop, one of the best in Paris, and the Académie du Vin, a wine shcool whose six-week courses are attended by the French Restaurant Association's chefs and sommeliers. Last week in Paris, at a formal wine tasting organized by Spurrier, the unthinkable happened: California defeated all Gaul.

The contest was as strictly controlled as the production of a Château Lafite. The nine French judges, drawn from an oenophile's *Who's Who*, included such high priests as Pierre Tari, secretary-general of the *Association des Grands Crus Classés,* and Raymond Oliver, owner of Le Grand Vefour restaurant and doyen of French culinary writers. The wines tasted were transatlantic cousins—four white Burgundies against six California Pinot Chardonnays and four Grands Crus Châteaux reds from Bordeaux against six California Cabernet Sauvignons.

Gallic Gems. As they swirled, sniffed, sipped and spat, some judges were instantly able to separate an imported upstart from an aristocrat. More often, the panel was confused. "Ah, back to France!" exclaimed Oliver from sipping a 1972 Chardonnay from the Napa Valley. "That is definitely California. It has no nose, " said another judge—after downing a Bâtard Montrachet '73. Other comments included such Gallic gems as "this is nervous and agreeable," "a good nose but not too much in the mouth," and "this soars out of the ordinary."

When the ballots were cast, the top-soaring red was Stag's Leap Wine Cellars' '72 from the Napa Valley, followed by Mouton-Rothschild '70, Haut-Brion '70 and Montrose '70. The four winning whites were, in order, Château Montelena '73 from Napa, French Meursault-Charmes '73 and two other Californians, Chalone '74 from Monterey County and Napa's Spring Mountain '73. The U.S. winners are little known to wine lovers, since they are in short supply even in California and rather expensive ($6 plus). Jim Barrett, Montelena's general manager and part owner, said: "Not bad for kids from the sticks."

- Odette Kahn, Editor of the magazines *La Revue du Vin de France* (Review of French Wine) and *Cuisine et Vins de France* (Food and Wine of France)
- Raymond Oliver, Chef and owner of Le Grand Véfour, a three-star Michelin restaurant with a fabulous wine cellar
- Pierre Tari, owner of Château Giscours and Secretary General of the Association des Grands Crus Classés, the organization of the French wines that were classified in 1855
- Christian Vannequé, Head Sommelier of the Tour d'Argent restaurant, a Michelin three-star restaurant that is probably the most famous in Paris
- Aubert de Villaine, Co-owner and Co-Director of the Domaine de la Romanée-Conti, one of Burgundy's most prized vineyards
- Jean-Claude Vrinat, owner of Taillevent restaurant, which had three Michelin stars, and who began his career as a sommelier

After they had tasted the wines and assigned the points, this is how it all added up:

Chardonnay:

- Chateau Montelena, 1973 — 132.0 points
- Meursault Charmes Roulot, 1973 — 126.5 points
- Chalone Vineyards, 1974 — 121.0 points
- Spring Mountain Vineyard, 1973 — 104.0 points

- Beaune Clos des Mouches, Joseph Drouhin, 1973 — 101.0 points
- Freemark Abbey Winery, 1972 — 100.0 points
- Bâtard-Montrachet, Ramonet-Prudhon, 1973 — 94.0 points
- Puligny-Montrachet Les Pucelles, Domaine Leflaive, 1972 — 89.0 points
- Veedercrest Vineyards, 1972 — 88.0 points
- David Bruce Winery, 1973 — 42.0 points

Cabernet Sauvignon:

- Stag's Leap Wine Cellars, 19731 — 127.5 points
- Château Mouton Rothschild, 1970 — 126.0 points
- Château Haut-Brion, 1970 — 125.5 points
- Château Montrose, 1970 — 122.0 points
- Ridge Vineyards Monte Bello, 1971 — 103.5 points
- Château Léoville-Las-Cases, 1971 — 97.0 points
- Mayacamas Vineyards, 1971 — 89.5 points
- Clos du Val Winery, 1972 — 87.5 points
- Heitz Cellars Martha's Vineyard, 1970 — 84.5 points
- Freemark Abbey Winery, 1969 — 78.0 points

This was the proof that all of the work of the winemakers in California to make great wines was paying off. The French wine experts could not tell the difference between the French and California wines! George Taber tells how one judge tasted the Bâtard-Montrachet and said, "This is definitely California," and how another exclaimed, "Ah, back to France," after tasting a Napa Valley Chardonnay.

In the article in *Time* Magazine on June 7, 1976, George Taber reported, "The unthinkable happened: California defeated Gaul."

I met Steven Spurrier years after the 1976 Paris Tasting when he came to my winery in Rutherford. In fact, I was talking to a group of guests and telling them the story of the Judgment of Paris when I realized that the man who had created the event was standing at the back of the group, listening. I told him that he was a man of great ideas and very good taste!

Over the years, I have been asked again and again, how had I done it? How could a little guy from a village in Croatia, the son of illiterate parents, beat the best French wine experts?

In a technical sense, I had done some things differently from the French. I made the Chardonnay using cold fermentation at about 45-50 degrees, which slowed the process down and preserved the natural aromas. The wine did not go through malolactic fermentation because I wasn't fond of the lactic aftertaste in French Chardonnays. Malic acid gave my Chardonnay a refreshing taste and crisp acidity so it paired well with food.

I had made about eight hundred cases of Chardonnay, fermented it slowly and aged it in French oak barrels for eight months. The 1972 and 1973 wines were both good but different in appearance, taste and character. The one-year-old oak barrels had given the 1973 more elegance and finesse with softer tannins.

It was the 1973 Chateau Montelena Chardonnay that went to Paris, but the 1972 Chardonnay, my first vintage at Chateau Montelena, while different was just as good, and not just because of the results of the May 27 and 28, 1975 San Diego tasting. Forty-one years later, for my ninetieth birthday on April 1, 2013, I held a celebration and invited friends and members of the press. We served everyone a taste of the 1972 Chardonnay I had made for Chateau Montelena. After forty-one years it was still a fine wine, with surprising freshness and depth. Obviously it had longevity. By this time in my life, I had almost lost count of the miracles!

Does discussing technique answer all the questions of what makes a wine great? Hardly. There is so much more! You must know your grapes, watch over them as they grow and ripen. You must pick them when the aromas and flavors are right, and then you must preserve these in your wine later. And there is passion and art, which come from the heart. Without art and passion, there is no life in the wines. Mother Nature, or perhaps we should say God, is the real winemaker after all, and we only learn to work together to make our wines.

The whole world was shocked by the results of the Judgment of Paris, and its effect was far-reaching, for it shattered the idea that only French soil could produce great wines. In California we had learned from the French and developed our own style. As a result of the 1976 Paris Tasting,

Patricia Gallagher and Steven Spurrier look on as Odette Kahn deliberates.

◈ Miljenko "Mike" Grgich

California, and Napa Valley in particular, had been recognized by the French as producing superior wines.

The Judgment of Paris energized the wine world. Not only in California but around the globe, winemakers realized that they too might have the *terroir* to produce premium wines. South Africa, Chile, Argentina, Italy, Australia and New Zealand were encouraged and joined the race to achieve greatness. My own home country, Croatia, had the potential to make fine wine and received stimulus from the Paris Tasting to make better wines.

Little did I know at the time that in 2010 one bottle of my 1973 Chardonnay would be auctioned in London for $11,325. I never imagined that the effect of the Judgment of Paris would be so powerful. My wine, along with the Stag's Leap Wine Cellars Cabernet Sauvignon, has been included in a book called *The Smithsonian's History of America in 101 Objects*. It is amazing to me that as an immigrant to this country, I would live to see my Chardonnay considered an "American object." I never could have imagined that one day the Smithsonian Institution National Museum of American History in Washington, D.C. would include in an exhibit two bottles of the winning wines from the Napa Valley, the first wines ever to be displayed in the museum. Or that also one day my little cardboard suitcase, my Croatian wine books, and my ebullioscope, which measures the alcohol content of a sample of wine, would all find a home in the Smithsonian. Even the French beret that I wore on my voyage to America is included in the exhibit. When I think back on how so many years before in Zagreb I had chosen, of all the hats on display, a French beret, I can only think that subconsciously I must have known something!

These honors were all far in the future. What did the victory mean for me in 1976? My life-long efforts had finally been recognized, and recognition can totally change the image you have of yourself. A piece of art may be great, but it needs someone to call it art. The Judgment of Paris gave me pride and security.

I knew my life was going to change. In 1976, I was fifty-three years old and had fifty years experience making wines. After the Judgment of Paris, I searched my soul for the reason I had come to America in the first place. Had I come to work for someone else or had I come to America to work for myself? I decided I had worked long enough for others. It was time to work for myself. This had been my dream when I left Croatia; now it was time to fulfill that dream.

Austin Hills and I breaking ground in Rutherford on Independence Day — July 4, 1977.

Chapter 14

The Founding of Grgich Hills

The Judgment of Paris had opened doors for me, and through them came many people offering me work at their wineries. But for me this would have been more of the same, of working for someone else. If I had wanted to do this all of my life, I could have stayed in Croatia and worked for the government. Perhaps I have a little artistic blood in my veins but I wanted to be on my own and make my wines the way my heart and soul told me to do it. For the first time since I had arrived in the Napa Valley, I finally felt close to attaining my dream.

I had finished my five-year contract at Chateau Montelena. I had some money. I sold my shares of Chateau Montelena, which were worth $50,000, and I also had the stock that Ernie Hahn had given me, which was now worth $45,000. My first plan was to buy two acres, make 2,000 cases of wine a year, build a winery and sales room, and sell the wine directly from there. An eighty-acre parcel was for sale in Rutherford, and I hoped that I might be able to buy two of these acres.

I had driven by this property for years, ever since I worked just up the road at Beaulieu Vineyard. This land was now owned by the Nestlé Company, which had purchased the old Beringer Winery in St. Helena in 1971.

A Swiss-based company, Nestlé was the first foreign company not involved in the wine business to invest in a California winery. I recall that one of their executives had asked André Tchelistcheff, "How much profit will we make in the wine business?"

André replied, "Don't think about how much you will make, but think of how much you are willing to lose."

In 1976, the company was selling off some of the land that had come with the purchase. Eighty acres was more than I could afford, but I could not buy two acres either, I discovered, because the land-zoning ordinance known as the Agricultural Preserve, which had passed in Napa County in 1968, required that any parcel of land could only be split into a minimum of twenty acres.

The Ag Preserve, which was the first of its kind in the United States, was the creation of people who were concerned about protecting the agricultural nature of the Napa Valley. They did not want to see the Napa County's farmland cut up into small parcels and converted to high-rise buildings and housing. This had already happened in the Santa Clara Valley, south of San Francisco, which today is Silicon Valley. To look at the land in Silicon Valley now, it is hard to imagine that it was once fields and farms, like Napa. So it was good that people in Napa had the foresight to preserve our greatest asset, the land for growing grapes.

So my idea of buying only two acres from that parcel did not materialize. I had $95,000 in my bank account. I came up with $5,000 more and so with $100,000 on hand I completed negotiations with Robert Pecota, representing the Nestlé Company, to purchase twenty acres of land in Rutherford as the site for a new winery.

The land was one of the lowest spots in the valley, so it was at risk of flooding and also captured the cold air rolling off the hills in spring that might frost the vines, but I liked its location in the middle of the valley on the main highway and its relatively low cost. My bookkeeper encouraged me to buy the property, despite the frost and flood dangers. "If you buy that land, you will make it a paradise," he said, knowing that I would work hard to make it productive.

My twenty acres were nothing but wild grass, yet it was land that I owned and I felt proud. I finally had a parcel that I could step on and say, "This land is mine."

My bookkeeper's prophecy was an accurate one. We installed frost protection fans and planted Chardonnay vines. Many years later, we would convert these vineyards to the Cabernet Sauvignon for which Rutherford is famous, producing a wonderful texture in wine called "Rutherford dust," but at this time we were still learning which parts of the valley were best for certain varieties. I would later plant my Chardonnay vines in the cooler climate to the south, in Carneros and American Canyon.

◦ Miljenko "Mike" Grgich

Now the question was how to build a winery.

Of all the people I had met who offered me jobs, Austin Hills interested me the most. He was a quiet man, thoughtful and well educated. He had studied at Stanford and Columbia universities, and as a member of the Hills Bros. Coffee family he had wide-ranging business experience. He had the money to invest since he and his sister, Mary Lee Strebl, had just sold the coffee company.

Austin was interested in wine. He already owned 155 acres of grapes where he grew Sauvignon Blanc, Chardonnay, and Johannisberg Riesling. Souverain Cellars made wine for him, which he sold under the Hills Cellars label. Austin, however, wanted to advance. He wanted to make "world-class" wine, he told me, and now I had the world-class reputation as the American who had beat the French.

As Austin and I talked, we realized that if we combined our strengths, it would benefit both of us. He could provide the money, and I the winemaking experience and knowledge. We could make "chateau-quality" wines, like those made at the great chateaux of France.

I felt it was a perfect match for success so I joined forces with Austin and his sister Mary Lee in a partnership.

While Austin and I were negotiating our partnership, I drove to San Francisco to meet with Theodore Kolb, an attorney who had been on the board of directors of Beaulieu Vineyard when I worked there. I told him that I had my twenty acres, and Austin and his sister Mary Lee Strebl could contribute $500,000.

"Mike, you are going to need $750,000 to build this winery," Mr. Kolb told me. "You are still $250,000 short."

I remembered my long-ago train ride across Canada, and my conversation with the man who had said immigrants could succeed if they started small and did all the work. I told Austin that if an American businessman said we needed $750,000, I knew we could do it on much less. I was not afraid of hard work, and I was willing to put everything I had, my time and energy and knowledge, into achieving this one thing, fulfilling my dream of establishing my own winery. I knew that we could succeed.

So we formed a partnership that many years later is still strong and thriving. Mr. Kolb worked out a business plan for a winery to produce ten thousand cases of wine a year, which I thought was the smallest amount we could produce and still be profitable. He was the trusted advisor to the partnership ever since, until his death in March 2015 at the age of 96. He had been ill the last year of his life, but he continued to work, literally, until the day he died.

As I prepared to leave Chateau Montelena, I brought with me two important elements in addition to the experience of creating a working winery. One was the old press, which I had used to make the 1972 and 1973 wines. Chateau Montelena needed a newer and larger press, and since it was no longer of use there, I bought it for my new winery.

The other important element was Gustavo Brambila. Gustavo had come to see me at Chateau Montelena asking for a job. Did I remember him? he asked. Many years before, he had been a little boy playing in the vineyards at Beaulieu Vineyard, where his father worked. I remembered that I had told his father to try to send at least one of his children to college. Gustavo had gone to the University of California, Davis, where he had been one of the first Mexican-American students to graduate with a degree in viticulture and enology. It was a happy occasion for me to give him his first job at a winery. Gustavo began by working in quality control at Chateau Montelena in 1976, and he was a great help. He went with me to the new winery and worked at Grgich Hills until 1999 before he went on to become general manager and winemaker at Peju Province Winery. In 1996, he formed a partnership with Thrace Bromberger to start his own winery, called Gustavo Thrace.

This is the way a man must progress, always moving forward and upward. Austin Hills and I were doing just that.

The winery project was underway. Austin and I decided that we would each choose a word to be combined together to create the new winery's name. Since my goal was to make chateau quality wines, I chose "Chateau" and Austin chose his name, "Hills." In February 1977, we submitted an application to the county for a new winery called Chateau Hills.

Although all the winery had at this point was a name, in April I went ahead and purchased the right to buy sixty tons of Chardonnay grapes from the 1977 harvest from the Disney family's Retlaw Vineyard, (Retlaw was Walter spelled backwards, in honor of Walt Disney) and all the Johannisberg Riesling I could pick from a 10-acre parcel owned by John

Hanna in Napa. This Riesling wine could be sold in six months and produce cash flow. The Chardonnay would take longer to be ready to sell.

Austin, meanwhile, hired an Austrian architect, who produced five sketches of wineries for $100. We chose the building with the most classic, cleanest-looking lines, and then his colleague Lou Gerhardt created the plans. In May 1977, we chose contractor John Kalua to build the winery.

While we waited for permission to begin to build the winery, we ran into our first hurdle. We needed to find water on the site, and my neighbor Dennis Gagetta was a "water witch" or dowser. A water witch uses two divining rods, usually copper sticks, to locate underground water. I hired him to help me locate underground water on my property. As we were walking over the land, he asked me, "Why do you need water?"

"I am going to build a little winery here," I said.

"How do you plan on getting to your winery?" he asked.

I was puzzled; what did he mean? Dennis explained, "I own the parcel between the railroad and Highway 29. You had better go talk to my lawyer."

My heart almost stopped. I raced to his lawyer in St. Helena to explain this calamity. If Dennis Gagetta owned the fifty feet of land between the railroad, at the edge of my property, and Highway 29, how could I build a winery if I had no way to get to it?

"Mike, calm down," the lawyer said, "This is not serious."

The lawyer knew me by reputation and he explained the

situation to me; I did indeed feel calmer. He told me that it was not even clear that Dennis Gagetta owned the property; he had never bought or inherited it but had just filed a claim with the county. In the end, it all worked out because Dennis Gagetta sold the house and the three-acre Cabernet Sauvignon vineyard next to my property to Mr. Richard Duarte. When I went to talk to Mr. Duarte and explained the problem with the entrance, he said, "No problem, Mike, you can use my driveway."

At the time it was just a gravel road, and so I proposed that I would pave a 24-foot wide driveway and we both could use it. Many years later when Mr. Duarte decided to sell the vineyard and house, I was able to buy it. His house now is home to the Grgich Hills Estate Legacy Room, containing displays and memorabilia that tell the history of our winery.

It is one of a few incidents I will always associate with the race to be ready for the grapes I had already bought for our winery.

Starting a new winery and brand means a thousand decisions have to be made but none are as visible as the name and the label. The permit for the winery had been made for the name Chateau Hills, but when Austin brought a friend to the winery and she saw that it was a simple stucco building with plywood walls and concrete floors, her response was, "That's NOT a chateau." Austin and I agreed to change the name of the winery. After some discussion, we decided to join our names to emphasize the family ownership and since "g" comes before 'h' in the alphabet, the name became Grgich Hills Cellar.

For the label, I suggested featuring Chardonnay grapes, since the Paris tasting had established my reputation with this varietal. I commissioned artist Sebastian Titus to design the label featuring a compact cluster of golden grapes. To show the family foundations of the winery, Austin and I contributed one design element each in the lower two corners of the label. He chose the rearing horse from his English family's crest, while I chose a red and white checkerboard crest, the coat of arms of my homeland, Croatia.

When I saw the design, I liked it, but being a perfectionist, I felt something was missing in the cluster of grapes.

I decided to approach my friend Margrit Biever (who would become Mrs. Robert Mondavi in 1980). Not only was she a wine expert, but she was also a fine artist. She looked at the cluster and immediately knew what to do. "Mike, you should make the grape clusters a little longer so the grapes form a triangle," she said. Sebastian Titus incorporated her suggestion in the artwork and we have used the same label throughout the years.

The label was perfect for white wines, but when I purchased Zinfandel wine for the 1976 vintage we had to make another decision. White grapes made no sense on a red wine label. I contacted Sebastian to redesign the label, and he said it would cost $3,000 that we did not have. I recalled many French producers proudly used black and white labels so I told the printer to simply convert the label to black and white. All of Grgich Hills' red wines were bottled with this stark label for 20 years, until a London wine lover wrote to me to complain that such a fine wine should not have such a cheap-looking label. By that time, my daughter, Violet, was head of the winery's sales and marketing, and she worked with Sebastian to create a new logo of purple Cabernet Sauvignon grapes to go on our red wine labels.

Austin and I decided to have our groundbreaking on July 4, 1977. As an immigrant who was grateful for the opportunities that America had offered me, I liked the idea that I was achieving my own freedom on Independence Day; I was fulfilling my lifelong dream. I was going to own my own winery.

A friend said to me, "You should have a sign." I went to a man in Calistoga and paid him $20 to paint a sign stating simply "Grgich Hills Cellar, Rutherford," which we planted into the ground by the spot we'd selected for our groundbreaking.

In the days leading up to the groundbreaking, I put four bottles of wine at the four corners of the foundation of the winery: 1958 Souverain Cabernet Sauvignon, a 1968 Beaulieu Georges de Latour Private Reserve Cabernet Sauvignon, a 1969 Robert Mondavi Private Reserve Cabernet Sauvignon, and a 1973 Chateau Montelena Chardonnay.

On July 4, 1977, we gathered about 50 relatives, neighbors and friends, including Robert and Michael Mondavi, to celebrate the birth of Grgich Hills Cellar. The first friends to arrive that day were our neighbor Bill Felsing and his family, who are still wine club members. My nephew, Father Anthony Domandich, blessed the land and the people who were

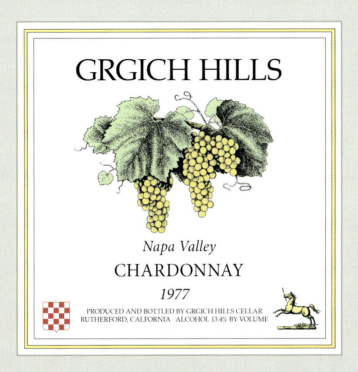

Our label

∽ Miljenko "Mike" Grgich

present. Austin Hills and I put our shovels into the earth and broke the ground for our new winery. My daughter Violet poured another bottle of 1973 Chardonnay into the hole we had dug to strengthen the foundation. It truly was my Independence Day too.

I had to find all of the equipment we would need, and we were on a tight budget. I had the old press that I had purchased from Chateau Montelena, but I was overburdened with how to find everything else — until it came to my mind that when wineries bought new equipment, they sold the old equipment. I began to search. We ordered new French oak barrels but the rest of the equipment I found all over the Napa and Sonoma Valleys. The crusher came from Sonoma, the grape hopper from Oakville Vineyards, the pump to move the crushed grapes was from Christian Brothers winery, and John Kalua built the hoist to lift the bins of grapes into the hopper. Not only would we save money, but we would be ready when the equipment was needed.

At the same time that I was purchasing equipment, I also needed to hire our first employees. It would be impossible to keep a keen eye on everything and so I was glad that Gustavo Brambila, my skilled assistant from Chateau Montelena, would be with me. The other position I needed to fill immediately was a bookkeeper and I hired Beverly Powell. Beverly continued to work for us for many years. She is the mother of Congressman Mike Thompson, who represents Napa and Sonoma Counties in the United States House of Representatives.

I also opened a business account with the local Wells Fargo Bank, and I am proud that we have had a business relationship ever since.

As I watched the slow progress of the construction, however, my confidence began to ebb. July was slipping away. Soon it would be August. In September my grapes would arrive. I was concerned about the pace of all the preparations and construction. What if I had nowhere for them to go?

By August I was so tense and scared, I went to my old friend Robert Mondavi.

"What's the problem, Mike?" he asked.

I said, "I am building a little winery, and I have bought sixty tons of Chardonnay but I don't think I will be ready to crush it."

He asked me, "When did you break ground?"

"July fourth," I said.

"Well," he said, "I broke ground on July 17, 1966 and I made it."

But he also offered that if the winery was not finished in September, I could crush my sixty tons of grapes at his winery. It was very generous of him because I knew that Robert Mondavi was crushing more grapes every year and he never had enough tank space for himself. He would need all of his own tank space. Still he wrote on a sheet of yellow legal paper that I could crush my grapes at his winery if I needed to, and he gave this promise to me. I am sorry now that I lost that piece of paper because it gave me peace of mind, and it

Celebrating my American Dream with
Robert Mondavi and Austin Hills
after breaking ground.

is proof of how a friend can help at a time of need. With that sheet of yellow paper in my hand, I knew then that my grapes would be safe.

We were getting close to harvest. Then, after waiting two months for a special electrical panel to be shipped from the East Coast, it finally arrived, and I was stunned to discover that they had sent the wrong one. This was a serious crisis: it was September 1, everything was ready, and we had no electricity!

I hired an electrician to track down the correct panel on the West Coast. Luckily, he found a panel in Salinas, and I arranged for the panel to be delivered and installed just before the grapes arrived.

Robert Mondavi had been right. We made it. The crusher/destemmer, press, and tanks were ready. They were framed by the new building, but the roof wasn't finished, so we put a plastic sheet over the rafters. On September 5, 1977, we crushed our first grapes at Grgich Hills. Appropriately, the first grapes we crushed were Chardonnay from John Hanna's vineyard.

Wherever people love wine and grape growing, they seem to love celebrating life, too. And, while harvest is the busiest time of the year, it's also the time to celebrate the results of many months of work tending the grapevines.

In Desne, our celebrations were quite simple. The big celebration was on St. Martin's Day, November 11, when the first public tasting of new wines took place. Everyone shared their new wines with their neighbors, along with lots of good food, singing and dancing.

∾ Miljenko "Mike" Grgich

It was a tradition and part of life in Desne that the first load of grapes would be blessed by a priest. This signaled the beginning of harvest. For Grgich Hills' first harvest, we asked Father George Aziz, the pastor of St. Helena Catholic Church, to officiate at our first Blessing of the Grapes. He blessed the grapes and the people and then he sprinkled the grapes and all those present with holy water, just as the priest used to do for my family when I was a child in Desne. It was a glorious day for me: I truly felt that I was in Paradise!

Grgich Hills has given thanks to God for the harvest every fall since that first blessing. The old saying, "You need great grapes to make great wine," is still true, which is one of the reasons why each year we invite a local priest to give a blessing of the first grapes to arrive at the winery. Afterwards, the employees and guests of Grgich Hills share a harvest lunch at the winery. We look back at what we have accomplished and look ahead to the wines yet to be made.

Every year since 1977, we also have had a Grgich Hills Fourth of July celebration. We celebrate both America and Croatia: we serve both American and Croatian foods, and we have American and Croatian music and dancing. This is because I, an immigrant from that faraway country, had, like many wanderers before me, made it in the New World. I had accomplished the goal of establishing a winery with my name on it. What better time to celebrate this than on the day that Americans toast their freedom and independence?

And what better way to honor the idea of patriotism than to combine the best of both nations?

CROATIAN FOLK DANCERS AT OUR PRE-RELEASE CLUB FESTIVAL AT AUSTIN'S HOME IN RUTHERFORD.

A Glass Full of Miracles

Passion for Success

I had no idea in April 1969 that later that year
I would make my first award-winning wine
at Robert Mondavi Winery.

In 2013, I enjoyed this bottle
of the 1969 Mondavi Cabernet.
It still tasted like a winner after all those years.

For my 90th birthday in 2013,
Jim Barrett sent this picture to me with this note:

"In 1972, forty years ago, I had the good fortune to hire Mike Grgich as Chateau Montelena's first Winemaker... Mike's reputation as a Master Winemaker was made when his 1973 Chardonnay won the Paris Tasting in 1976. Happy Birthday, Mike!"

From left to right: Ernie Hahn, Jim Barrett and Lee Paschich, standing behind me.

With longtime friends Margrit and Robert Mondavi on the occasion of my 80th birthday.

Standing in front of the old press at Chateau Montelena.

George Tabor in back on the left carefully observing the wines being poured for the judges on May 24, 1976.

FATHER ANTHONY DOMANDICH OFFICIATING
AT THE GRGICH HILLS CELLAR GROUNDBREAKING.

My daughter Violet pouring a bottle of the 1973 Chateau Montelena Chardonnay at the southeast corner of the foundation, for luck.

My brother-in-law Vide Domandich at our groundbreaking.

Who needs a roof? We are all ready to crush grapes. Through the door you can see the press used for the 1973 Chardonnay. I purchased it from Chateau Montelena.

Our first Blessing of the Grapes at Grgich Hills on September 5, 1977.

Austin Hills and I watch as the hoist lifts our first load of Chardonnay into the hopper.

I'm still bursting with joy from the news of the
Great Chicago Chardonnay Shootout at the
1980 Southern California Wine Writers wine tasting.

Austin Hills and I on the front porch of his home in Rutherford celebrating our success with a glass of Chardonnay.

OUR NEW FRONT DOOR —
WELCOME TO GRGICH HILLS CELLAR!

Chapter 15

The King of Chardonnay

My American dream of freedom and being able to run a free enterprise became a reality in 1977. Now I had not only my own piece of land in Napa Valley but also a winery where I could use all I had learned from my father, who had learned from his forefathers. I could use all the knowledge I learned from the University of Zagreb and the University of California, Davis, from Lee Stewart, Brother Timothy, André Tchelistcheff and Robert Mondavi. I could draw on my life experiences, from that of a fourteen-year-old shopkeeper trying to collect payment for his bills to that of a mature winemaker trying to create a winery in an old ghost winery, Chateau Montelena. Would I be lucky? I remembered one of my mottos: "When preparation meets opportunity — that is luck."

I overcame all of my trepidations about starting a new winery as I made my first vintage at Grgich Hills Cellar. That year we bought 100 tons of Chardonnay grapes, the original sixty from Napa County and forty more from Sonoma. I also bought thirty tons of Riesling grapes to make a wine that could be sold in six months. The Chardonnay would take longer.

To generate immediate sales, the partnership purchased bottled 1976 Chardonnay and 1976 Riesling from Austin Hills' own label, Hills Cellars. The 1976 Zinfandel bulk wine that I purchased was aged at the winery and scheduled to be released in 1979.

On November 1, 1977, we opened our tasting room and began selling Austin's wines. I bought a table for ten dollars to use as the tasting room bar. That was a good investment: over the years, I have sold millions of dollars of wine over that table!

My plan for the winery's growth was careful and conservative. At first we sold wine only at the winery. Next I took wine to sell in St. Helena, the nearest town, just north of Rutherford. When it sold well there, I ventured to Napa, thirteen miles to the south. When this was successful, we went as far as San Francisco, forty-five miles away.

I knew that it could take anywhere from five to ten years for a winery to become profitable. That first year we lost $49,000 because we had only been open two months and our expenses had been great. But in 1978 we regained everything, and we earned a profit. We have earned a profit every year since then. We have never had a loss, and we don't owe the bank any money. We even have money in the bank. This is, and I think anyone in the wine industry would agree, quite a miracle.

But we had a long way to go before we reached this point in our business. The early sales proved to me that I was on the right track with my goal to make wines that had balance, elegance and longevity. People liked them; they were buying them, especially my Chardonnay. I was soon to get more confirmation that my Grgich Hills Chardonnay was a success.

In 1980, Chris Cunningham, president of the Orange County Wine Society in Costa Mesa, in Southern California, wrote to me asking if the winery would submit three bottles of wine for the annual wine competition at the Orange County Fair. He told me that this area had become a major center of wine consumption in the U.S. and that since 1976 this wine competition had been part of the Orange County Fair, with a goal of developing the appreciation and enjoyment of wine as part of our everyday culture.

The Orange County Fair had grown each year and by 1980 it included thirteen different varieties in its wine judging: Chenin Blanc, in both dry and off-dry styles, Gewürztraminer, Sauvignon Blanc, Chardonnay, Blanc de Noir, Petite Sirah, Cabernet Sauvignon, Pinot Noir, Zinfandel, Dry Late Harvest Zinfandel, Sweet Late Harvest Zinfandel and Dry Sherry. All the wines were judged in a blind tasting by professionals — vintners, winemakers and other winery representatives — who traveled to Orange County for the competition. They used a 20-point Davis modified rating system that was approved by the industry. All of the wines were sold in local markets.

The wines were judged in three price classifications: inexpensive, moderate and premium; this was for purposes of consumer-comparison benefit. I submitted the Grgich Hills 1977 Chardonnay, which at $12.00 per bottle in stores was in the premium category. The panel judging my wine was made up of Dawnine Sample of Domaine Chandon, Richard Arrowood of Chateau St. Jean, Richard Elwood of Llords & Elwood Winery and Warren Winiarski of Stag's Leap Wine Cellars. They gave it a gold medal. It was the first gold medal for Grgich Hills.

An even bigger competition lay ahead: The Great Chicago Chardonnay Showdown.

In 1980, Craig Goldwyn, the wine columnist for the *Chicago Tribune*, worked with Schaefer's Wines and Liquors of Skokie, Solomon's of Chicago and Sola's of Riverdale to organize a grand tasting of Chardonnay. Winemakers from around the world were invited to submit their wine to this historic competition. In all, 221 of the best Chardonnays from around the world were collected in Chicago. It was the largest blind tasting ever held of wines made from a single varietal. In his article titled "The Great Chicago Chardonnay Showdown," Goldwyn recounted: "They were all made from Chardonnay grapes, the grape that makes the best dry white wines in the world. They came from not only France and California, but from New York, Washington, and Bulgaria, to name a few."

The judges were professionals from Chicago, New York and Michigan. The panelists included:

- Edward Robert Brooks, "Gourmet on the Go," Chicago
- Patrick W. Fegan, Wine Columnist, *Chicago* magazine
- Joseph Glunz, Vice President, Louis Glunz, Inc., Lincolnwood, Illinois

- Myrna Greenspan, Sales Representative, Wine House Division, Union Liquor Company, Chicago, Illinois
- John Hart, Partner, Chicago Wine Company, Wood Dale, Illinois
- Gerald A. Hirsch, President, Custom House Wine Merchants, Skokie, Illinois
- Dana Keeler, Cellarmaster at Bully Hill Vineyards in Hammondsport, New York
- Norb Mizwicki, Wine Instructor, Park Ridge, Illinois
- Myron Nightingale, Winemaker of Beringer Vineyards in St. Helena, California
- Neil O'Brien, Wine Director and Sommelier, La Tour Restaurant, Chicago, Illinois
- Leonard Olson, Wine Master, Tabor Hill Vineyards, Buchanan, Michigan
- Dr. Richard Peterson, Winemaker at the Monterey Vineyard, Gonzales, California
- Max Ponder, Wine Director, Armanetti Wines and Liquors, Chicago, Illinois
- Sterling Pratt, Wine Director, Schaefer's Wines and Liquors, Skokie, Illinois
- Laurence Ratner, Wine Director, Connoisseur Wines Ltd., Chicago, Illinois
- Maurice L. Ross, Jr., Vice President, Wine House Division, Union Liquor Company, Chicago, Illinois
- George Schaefer, Proprietor, Schaefer's Wines and

> Miljenko "Mike" Grgich

    Liquors, Skokie, Ilinois

- Ron Senoff, Proprietor, Red Arrow Wines and Liquors, Chicago, Illinois
- Howard Silverman, Wine Consultant, Sam's Wine Warehouse, Chicago, Illinois
- Leonard Solomon, Solomon's Wines and Liquors, Chicago, Illinois
- Jim Steele, Wine Director, Sola's Liquors, Riverdale, Illinois
- Dennis Styck, Sales Representative, Wine House Division, Union Liquor Company, Chicago, Illinois
- Nanci Versino, Wine Consultant, Chicago, Illinois
- Rick Ward, Midwest Regional Manager, Robert Mondavi Winery
- Ed Wawszkiewicz, Microbiologist and former Consulting Enologist to Mt. Eden Vineyards, Chicago, Illinois
- Julius Wile, Julius Wile and Sons Co., Scarsdale, New York

    The tasting took place in two parts. The first step was the "showdown by price," with five panels of five judges each. Next, ten of the judges reconvened at the "shootout" to review the top nineteen scoring wines, regardless of price. The winning wines of the Great Chicago Chardonnay Showdown were:

- Chardonnay Sonoma 1977, Grgich Hills Cellar
- Beaune "Close des Mouches" 1978, J. Drouhin
- Pinot Chardonnay, Napa Valley 1974, Heitz Cellars

- Chardonnay Alexander Valley 1977, Simi Winery
- Chardonnay California 1978, Chateau Montelena
- Meursault Premier Cru "Genevrières" 1978, A. Ropiteau
- Chassagne Montrachet "Morgeaot" 1978, Ponnelle
- Chardonnay Sonoma 1978, Dry Creek Vineyard
- Chevalier-Montracher 1978, M. Niellon
- Puligny-Montrachet 1978, L. Jadot
- Chardonnay 1978, Inglenook Vineyards
- Chardonnay "Claire de Lune" 1978, Hacienda Wine Cellars
- Macon Blanc Villages 1978, L. Jadot
- Bâtard-Montrachet 1978, M. Niellon
- Petit Chablis 1979, Lamblin
- Macon Villages 1978, G. Duboeuf
- Pouilly-Fuissé 1978, Ch. de Beauregard
- Macon "St. Louis" Chardonnay 1977, B&G
- Bourgogne Blanc Supérieur 1977, DeLoisy

When it was all over, "...the winner and still champion was Miljenko 'Mike' Grgich (Grgich Hills 1977 Chardonnay, Sonoma $18)," Craig Goldwyn wrote. "The first wine his new winery produced has again topped top French competitors."

I read his words with a great feeling of satisfaction: "Grgich had also the top-rated wine in 1976 when a respected Paris merchant matched six of California's Chardonnays against four of France's most famous white Burgundies," he wrote.

"In the giddy atmosphere of the American bicentennial, the Grgich victory was proclaimed by practically every newspaper in the United States as the coming of age of American wine."

Another account of both the Chicago Showdown and the Orange County Fair came from a journalist closer to home.

In his article "Chardonnay Showdown" in the *Vallejo Times-Herald* dated December 7, 1980, wine writer Jerry Mead wrote about the Chicago Showdown and Orange County Fair Tasting:

"Unless you subscribe to *The Chicago Tribune*, chances are you haven't heard about 'The Great Chicago Chardonnay Shootout and Showdown.'"

After describing the contest, he added, "The winning wine is really part of a very special story . . . back in 1976, a fellow named Steven Spurrier (now famous for his Taylor wine commercials), a little known wine merchant in Paris, organized a comparative tasting between a number of French wines produced from the Chardonnay grape and a similar number produced in California. The judges were all French.

"A California wine won that tasting, resulting in international publicity, a number of the French judges attempting to retract their scores, and no doubt, offers to turn in their taste-vins in shame. I exaggerate only a little.

"The winning wine was a Chardonnay from Napa Valley's Chateau Montelena, and the winemaker was a nice little man with a name that drove typesetters crazy, Miljenko 'Mike' Grgich.

Chicago Tribune magazine,
November 9, 1980

∽ Miljenko "Mike" Grgich

"Well, Grgich did it again, only this time for his own new winery, Grgich Hills, also of Napa Valley, and this the very first Chardonnay produced under the winery's new roof. And just in case you have no faith in wine judging, might I point out that this very same 1977 Grgich Hills Chardonnay was a gold medal winner in the premium price range at this year's Orange County Fair. Winning the top award at one highly competitive judging can be a fluke, but top honors at two such events should convince even the most cynical."

In his *Chicago Tribune* column, "The Grape Vine," Craig Goldwyn wrote a piece titled "The Best Chardonnay in the World" that was published on Monday, November 17, 1980. For it, he asked me, "What is your secret? How were you able to make the best Chardonnay in the world?"

I replied, and he quoted me: "Tender loving care, keeping the wine as natural as possible. Not processing, not centrifuging, not filtering."

I explained, "Many people think that to have the perfect wine, you have to have a computer. I forget computers. I baby my wines. I am really a wine sitter, not a wine maker. I give them a good environment and they develop into good wines. I think that for me it is more art than science, but I have the science in my head if I need it."

That was how I felt in 1980, and though it is still true, I would say today that I am an artist winemaker as well as a wine sitter. I have that article written by Craig Goldwyn framed and hanging in the Legacy Room at Grgich Hills Estate.

Garnering the first place in both the Great Chicago

Chardonnay Showdown and the Orange County Fair was proof that the Judgment of Paris had not been an accident, and I discovered that I was being affectionately called "the King of Chardonnay." Imagine that — to be called King! I felt on top of the world.

After the Great Chicago Showdown, we had to put a limit on the number of cases any one person could buy of Grgich Hills Chardonnay. It would be three cases a year until we could increase our production to meet the demand. It took us fifteen years to do that.

As Grgich Hills' reputation grew, we added to our portfolio of wines. In 1979, we released our first Sauvignon Blanc, which I called Fumé Blanc, since it was made in the style that I had learned when I worked for Robert Mondavi. He had created this name for a wine made from Sauvignon Blanc, because, although this is the main white grape grown in Bordeaux, it did not have a good reputation in the United States at the time, where many wines made from it were of inferior quality. The name was inspired by the "Pouilly Fumé" wines in Loire Valley — crisp elegant Sauvignon Blanc wines, with the "Fumé" meaning that it was aged in oak. Robert also was concerned that Americans would not buy a wine called Sauvignon Blanc because it was hard to pronounce.

In 1984 we released our first Cabernet Sauvignon, from our 1980 vintage. This "king of red grapes" is the one most widely grown in Napa Valley, where the growing conditions, the dry hot summers and long ripening time, suit it well.

The next wine I would add, in 1994, was a sweet wine,

which I named Violetta, after my daughter Violet. The final wine to our line-up at Grgich Hills came in 2002 when we released our first Merlot, from the 1999 vintage.

Meanwhile, events were taking place that continued to astonish me: In 1981 the White House served our 1979 Chardonnay at a dinner for King Juan Carlos of Spain. The next year President Reagan took the same vintage to France to serve to the French President François Mitterrand at the American Embassy. In 1983, our 1978 Chardonnay was served to Queen Elizabeth II of Great Britain during her visit to California when she had dinner at the home of Donald Kennedy, president of Stanford University.

What an amazing thing it was for me to know that kings and queens and presidents were drinking and enjoying a wine that I, a shepherd from a little village in Croatia, had made.

35 Years Later

In 1980 when the Great Chicago Chardonnay Showdown took place, we were so busy at the winery that we hardly took time to celebrate this victory, and in consequence, it is not nearly as well known as the 1976 Judgment of Paris tasting. This is why, 35 years after the event, we took the time to celebrate in grand style the tasting that proved to me that I could make "the best Chardonnay in the world."

In 2015 two celebrations took place, one in Chicago and one in Napa Valley. In Chicago, Mayor Rahm Emanuel declared May 7, 2015 the "Great Chicago Chardonnay

Showdown Day," and we hosted a gala dinner at the Signature Room at the 95th Floor at John Hancock Center in Chicago. An honored guest was Craig Goldwyn, the wine writer for the *Chicago Tribune*, who in 1980 had organized and served as a judge at the Showdown.

Croatia celebrated with me: among the guests were His Excellency, The Most Reverend Blase J. Cupich, Archbishop of Chicago, who is of Croatian descent; Sam Toia, President of the Illinois Restaurant Association; Josip Paro, Croatia's Ambassador to United States; Jelena Grčić Polić, Consul General of the Republic of Croatia in Chicago; and fellow Croatians Toni Kukoč and Ivica Dukan of the Chicago Bulls. My daughter Violet was thrilled to accept the key to the city of Chicago and read a proclamation from the mayor at this proud moment for me and for Croatian-Americans.

Back in Napa at the winery, Violet and I welcomed 130 guests to a second gala party, and this time joining our celebration was our U.S. Congressman Mike Thompson, who presented me with a congressional declaration marking the 35th anniversary of the tasting. State Assembly Member Bill Dodd, Napa County Supervisor Diane Dillon, and Calistoga Mayor Chris Canning were also among my friends at the event. Another special guest was my long-time friend Tony Butala, a fellow Croatian who is a founding member of the musical group The Lettermen, who serenaded me with "The Impossible Dream" and my favorite Croatian songs. Croatia may be a little country but we know how to share our joys in a great way.

DINNER

Loup de mer flambé au fenouil
Riz au safran

Selle d'agneau Richelieu
Bouquetière de légumes

Salade à l'estragon
Brillat-savarin

Bavarois Plombière Coulis de framboise

Grgich Hills
Chardonnay 1979

Martha's Vineyard
Heitz
Cabernet Sauvignon 1974

Domaine Chandon
Brut Special Reserve

AMERICAN EMBASSY RESIDENCE

Paris, France
Thursday, June 3, 1982

**Le Président de la République Française
and Madame Mitterrand**

March 30, 1983

Dear Mr. Grgich:

Nancy and I were very pleased to learn about your generous contribution to the festivities in honor of Her Majesty Queen Elizabeth II. The visit was a memorable occasion for all of us, and we deeply appreciate your gesture of friendship and goodwill.

With our warm appreciation and best wishes,

Sincerely,

Ronald Reagan

Mr. Miljenko Grgich
c/o Grgich Hills Cellar
Post Office Box 450
Rutherford, California 94573

∞ Miljenko "Mike" Grgich

Susan Ungaro, president of the James Beard Foundation, was at the Napa dinner too, and spoke about the Miljenko "Mike" Grgich American Dream Scholarship we created in partnership with the James Beard Foundation, which gives deserving young wine professionals an opportunity to succeed just as I had been able to succeed in my adopted country that has given me so much. It was good to be with my friends from over the decades, and with my daughter, who was doing so much to continue our success at Grgich Hills.

But perhaps the greatest thing for me was that we still had some of the 1977 Grgich Hills Chardonnay that had been named best in the world, and we opened the bottles at a tasting for the media. It was still good. Now, that is a victory worth a celebration — or, in this case, two!

I was honored to have Congressman Mike Thompson, whose mother Beverly Powell was my first bookkeeper at Grgich Hills, present me with a Congressional Record which honored me and my achievements, during our celebration on May 14, 2015 of the 35th anniversary of the Great Chicago Chardonnay Showdown at Grgich Hills Estate.

An original old Cabernet vine, planted in 1959 in our Yountville vineyard.

Chapter 16

A String of Pearls

When we started Grgich Hills, Austin Hills and I had almost nothing except for a bare patch of land in Rutherford and my vision of what the wine should be. At first, we bought most of our grapes, but as the winery became profitable, we were able to invest in buying our own land.

Why is that important? Because great wines begin with the best grapes. You can make an adequate wine from poor quality grapes, but that has never been my goal. I wanted always to strive for the best. We have many fine grape growers in the Napa Valley who produce premium fruit, but when you own the vineyards and farm them yourself, you can control the quality of your grapes at the source, from pruning through harvest.

I should really say that you and Mother Nature have control. Each year, you never know what surprises She has in store for a farmer. Since I was a boy, I had learned to have the utmost respect for Mother Nature and her gifts: sunshine, rain,

∾ Miljenko "Mike" Grgich

drought, fog and heat waves. She always has the final word!

Our first land purchase in Rutherford was originally part of a large land grant that had been given to Mexican General Mariano Vallejo in the 1820s. In 1831, Gen. Vallejo deeded a large parcel, called the Caymus Rancho, to George Yount, who was the first non-native settler in the Napa Valley. (The town of Yountville was named in his honor in 1867.)

The twenty acres of land in Rutherford that I purchased for the winery site and Grgich Hills' first vineyard had been planted with Chardonnay grapes, but the knowledge and experience we were gaining in those pioneering years of the 1960s had taught us much about the *terroir* of Napa County. This is a small valley, but from north to south it has an extraordinary range of soils and climate differences. It was soon clear to me that Chardonnay, which loves cool climates, would do better in the cool and windy Carneros and American Canyon regions to the south, while sun-loving Cabernet Sauvignon would thrive in Rutherford where the now-famous "Rutherford Dust" soil suits it. After I found good land for our Chardonnay, I had the Rutherford vineyard replanted to primarily Cabernet Sauvignon with one acre of Petit Verdot, a grape used in Bordeaux blends.

As both the winery and the Napa Valley prospered, I was finally able to purchase some land that I had been watching since I'd first arrived in the Napa Valley.

In 1958, I did not have a car for three years so I often rode the Greyhound Bus that traveled up and down the valley. The route went by a vineyard in Yountville that I came to know well, near Hopper Creek, not far from where the first grapes were planted in the Napa Valley by George Yount.

These Cabernet Sauvignon vines interested me very much. They were from the Inglenook clone Cabernet Sauvignon, also known as Niebaum Cabernet Sauvignon #29, from the famous Inglenook Vineyard in Rutherford. They were planted on the hearty St. George rootstock, which is able to resist phylloxera. I felt that the vineyard was one of the valley's finest, with ideal sun exposure and loamy topsoil over pebbly gravel, perfect for drainage.

This is why when I saw bulldozers tearing up these vines I felt like someone was pulling out my teeth. I learned that Highway 29, one of the two main arteries that run from north to south in the valley (the other is Silverado Trail against the eastern hills) was being redirected to go straight through the vineyard, and not through the town of Yountville as before. These grapevines were in the way, so they had to go. I was devastated and I decided that one day I would buy what remained of that vineyard, which was eventually replanted in 1959.

When it was offered for sale, I tried to buy it but was outbid. In all, I tried four times before I was finally successful. In August 1984, Grgich Hills became the owner of 79 acres of prime Cabernet vineyard in Yountville. This included the old vineyard planted in 1959 and a beautiful white Victorian mansion that was one hundred years old.

This house was a bonus, but I liked it very much because, in addition to being a graceful and charming building, it told a

⁓ Miljenko "Mike" Grgich

story. George Yount had sold the land to a man named Charles Hopper, who gave four acres to the creation of the road that became Highway 29. In 1871 he sold the remaining 112 acres to Thomas Fawver who planted grapes and in 1885 built the house that came to be known as the Fawver House.

I moved from St. Helena in 1985 to live in this Victorian, which was, beyond measure, the nicest house I'd ever lived in. Living there showed me how far I had come since I'd first arrived in the Napa Valley and bought my first house, the smallest, cheapest house in St. Helena, the one with the crooked floors. I was beginning to feel like an American!

I especially loved the views from the upstairs windows — the vineyard was the best in the valley and I was almost certain that I would be able to make wonderful wines, particularly from the vines that were planted in 1959 to the Inglenook clone on St. George rootstock.

The Fawver House became my home for the next sixteen years. I had plenty of room for visitors in this house, but perhaps the most memorable ones were the uninvited guests who moved in and stayed: these were the bees that made their home in the eaves of the mansion. I had to move them from the eaves to their own hive, but they remained on the property — my tenants who pay no rent except their golden honey.

I love the wonderful, old vines in this vineyard. They are, I believe, the second oldest Cabernet Sauvignon vines in the valley. Old vines often produce lower yields but in return the fruit is of exceptional richness and quality. The fruit from these vines was so intense in their flavors that I decided they

This beautiful Victorian home was built in 1885 and sits in the middle of our Yountville vineyard, now known as "Violet's Vineyard." I lived here from 1985 — 2001 and our annual Wine Club Festival takes place here on every 4th of July weekend.

Our Carneros Vineyard, now known as "Mary Lee's Vineyard".

were worthy of their own special label. We fermented and bottled the best lots separately and made the first vintage of the Yountville Selection Cabernet Sauvignon in 1991. That first vintage and many others over the years have won great praise, and they deserve it. Old vines, just like old people, are capable of a quality that the young cannot yet accomplish, the wisdom that only age can bring. Wine and women improve with age — never underestimate them!

My first Grgich Hills Chardonnays were a blend of purchased grapes from John Hanna of Napa and from the Disney family's Retlaw Vineyard in Yountville but as soon as I could afford it, I began to search for vineyards for Chardonnay.

I was especially pleased with the grapes I bought from John Hanna, and so I looked to the Carneros region. Carneros, which straddles Napa and Sonoma Counties at the edge of the San Francisco Bay, was once part of the Rincon Los Carneros Spanish Land Grant. This wind-swept land had been home to sheep ranches, which gave the area its name — Los Carneros means "the rams" in Spanish. Here, the cooling influence of the Pacific Ocean and the area's shallow but dense soil allow the grapes longer hang-time on the vine to develop more complex flavors.

Eventually, I found a parcel that the Sebastiani family wanted to sell. It had been planted as a vineyard previously but it was bare land when Grgich Hills purchased 101 acres in 1989.

Before planting the vineyard, I had a backhoe dig a pit to see exactly what types of soils were there. The pit revealed a two-foot layer of fine brown soil with almost pure sand underneath. I used this knowledge later when the vines we planted on AxR1 rootstock soon showed signs of phylloxera, an insect related to aphids that feeds on the roots of grape vines. I cut back on irrigation, driving the vine roots deep into the sand to find water. Phylloxera is unable to survive in sand and this allowed the vines to remain productive. Today, Grgich Hills farms seventy-three acres of Chardonnay there as well as a few acres of Merlot, Sauvignon Blanc, and Cabernet Franc, all planted on the Napa side of the Carneros appellation.

With the success of its plantings in Carneros, we looked next to American Canyon, in the southern-most section of Napa Valley. In 1996 we purchased 203 acres just east of Carneros in the foothills of Sulphur Springs Mountains. This site, once part of General Vallejo's Rancho Suscol land grant, had never been farmed but was used only for grazing cattle. American Canyon is slightly cooler than Carneros, with even stronger winds that reduce the vines' vigor; this results in high quality, concentrated fruit.

The soils here are diverse, and range from sandy to sandy-loam and clay to clay-loam over slate, all good for grapes. The site's rolling hills ensure that rain drains naturally away from the vines — a highly prized attribute since vines do not like wet feet. Our American Canyon vineyards became the largest Grgich Hills' holdings and were planted primarily with Chardonnay and Sauvignon Blanc, and some Merlot. In the coolest blocks of the vineyard, we planted Riesling, Sauvignon Blanc and Gewürztraminer. Here, when conditions are right, we can harvest grapes affected with *botrytis*, the "noble rot" that produces an intensely flavored sweet "Late Harvest" wine, which I named Violetta after my daughter, Violet.

I had one more purchase to make. Back in the 1970s, when I worked at Chateau Montelena, I had come to know a vineyard on the western side of Calistoga where I had purchased grapes. In part of this vineyard grew Zinfandel vines that were more than 100 years old. No one knew who had planted the oldest vines; newer plantings had been budded over the century old vines. This vineyard produced some of the best Zinfandel I had ever tasted — here again is the value of age! I patiently waited until the vineyard came on the market in 1997 and purchased it. In 1998, we made the first vintage of Miljenko's Old Vine Zinfandel using only the fruit from these vines, which we released in 2001.

It was a beautiful place, peaceful and serene, with oak and pine trees surrounding the vineyards. To the east was a grand view of Mount St. Helena. Here, with the Zinfandel and the mountain, I felt a deep connection to my homeland, to Desne in Croatia. I named it Miljenko's Vineyard, using my Croatian name. More than any other place, this vineyard represented a return to my roots. Here were Zinfandel vines, which I believed then and now knew for certain, had come from Croatia, like me. And they grew in the shadow of a mountain that reminded me of Babina Gomila, which I had climbed as a child in Desne. I decided I would build a home here, on a wooded site just above the vineyard, looking out at Mt. St. Helena.

It took two decades to find and plant our vineyards, but

∽ Miljenko "Mike" Grgich

in the end we had expanded our vineyards from twenty acres in 1977 to 366 in 2003. We had created what I called "a string of pearls," a collection of prime quality vineyards, all of them dotting Napa Valley from north to south like precious gems. We could now grow all the grapes for our wines, although it would not be until 2007 that we decided to change the name of our winery to reflect this milestone of being completely estate grown. That year we became Grgich Hills Estate.

To return to the subject of the 1980s: this was a decade of growth for the whole valley. For Austin and me the policy of slow and steady growth worked, but Napa Valley was changing swiftly. Land prices were rising as more and more people rushed to build wineries and get into the wine business.

Violet had grown up accompanying me into the vineyards and cellars. When she wasn't in school in the summers, she worked at the winery. I knew that one day she would take over the leadership of Grgich Hills Estate and so I wanted her to learn every aspect of a winery, from cellar work and doing laboratory analyses to working in accounting and in the tasting room. I remember she used to complain that I insisted she hand wash the glasses from the tasting room. "Why don't we buy a dishwasher?" she asked me. "It would be much more efficient!"

I had not told her very much at this time about my early years, and it was much later that she learned about my lonely years in Canada, when I was waiting and trying to get to America. When she heard how I had started in Canada by learning how to dry glasses, she said to me, "Now I understand why you made me wash the glasses!"

The view from my porch overlooking my "Miljenko's Vineyard" in Calistoga. Mt. St. Helena stands watch over it just as Babina Gomila did over my Croatian home in Desne.

∾ Miljenko "Mike" Grgich

In 1983, Violet left for college at the University of California, Davis. She had always had a talent for music. When she was only two years old, I took a piece of bamboo and made a little flute for her, such as we used to make when I was a boy in Desne. She would try to play music with it but one time it nearly led to a calamity because she fell with it in her mouth and it went through her bottom lip into the roof of her mouth. This had happened just as I arrived home for lunch, and I found my wife and my sister Ljubica, who was visiting from Croatia, in a great panic. Luckily we were able to rush Violet to the doctor, who removed the pipe, and she was fine. In spite of this, Violet retained her interest in music, and so at Davis, she studied music as well as enology and she went on to earn a master's degree in music at the University of Indiana.

While Violet was at school, our family grew to include an important new member: my grandnephew, Ivo Jeramaz, the grandson of my sister Neda.

Like me, Ivo grew up helping make wine with his family in Croatia. He didn't, however, plan to become a winemaker. He went to the University of Zagreb to study engineering, and after he earned a master's degree, he dreamed of coming to California to work.

I was able to help him, and in 1986 he arrived in Napa Valley. This was a joyous time for me, to have a relative interested in wine, fun and good times. I remember many a night waiting up for him at the Victorian house — sometimes seeing him creeping home and trying to climb through a window because he knew he was late.

Blending generations — having fun with my daughter Violet and grandnephew Ivo.

∞ Miljenko "Mike" Grgich

Was it inevitable? Ivo became fascinated with winemaking and changed his mind about his career. I gave him a job washing barrels, and he worked his way up through many jobs in the winery to become a winemaker. For me, it was important that he follow the family tradition that sees winemaking as both a science and an art.

During his more than two decades at Grgich Hills, Ivo has increased his responsibility, learning how to make wine using art and ancient wisdom, supported by the tools of science and technology. If you ask him, he will be the first to tell you that there's no job in the winery or vineyard that he has not done, and not just for one day either; he has really worked at each job.

In the cellar, another valuable person was Gary Ecklin, who joined Grgich Hills in 1981 as chief enologist. An important contribution he made was to bring in OXOline, an ingenious system for stacking and rotating oak barrels to manage the delicate "*sur lie*" aging process with even greater care. For our white wines, the cellar crew uses the system to regularly rotate each 60-gallon oak barrel, gently stirring up the "lees," the deposits of yeast and other particles that naturally sink to the bottom of a barrel. This gives the wine additional complexity and body without exposing the wine to air.

In 1988, I was pleased when Violet joined the winery as a full-time employee. There had been ups and downs throughout the valley in the 1980s, and in many vineyards phylloxera had struck so they had to be replanted. Wine sales were always affected by the nation's economy so there were some dips during the deep recession of the early 1980s, but for the most part the wine industry in the Napa Valley was strong and growing and I was happy to have my daughter share in that with me. We had survived our first decade as a winery and were thriving.

What was next? I would not have imagined that soon, instead of bringing my relatives from Croatia, I would be going home.

My grandnephew Ivo Jeramaz in our Rutherford Vineyard working closely with Mother Nature.

St. Mark's Church in Zagreb, dating from the late 1400s. The tiles on the roof show the coats of arms of the Triune Kingdom of Croatia, Slavonia and Dalmatia (left), and of Zagreb (right).

CHAPTER 17

RETURN TO CROATIA

On November 9, 1989 came a world event that again would change my life. In Germany, the Berlin Wall that had divided the city between the Communist East and the free West was torn down. This symbol of the Iron Curtain that had isolated Communist Europe from the world was destroyed. The Soviet Union and its Communist satellites were in turmoil. One by one, countries like Czechoslovakia, Hungary, Poland, Bulgaria and Romania became free again. So did Croatia.

In Croatia the desire for freedom was strong. During my long years away from my homeland, I had always been in touch with many people there, friends and family. Concern for them was part of my life, but it had seemed that what I could do was help people like my nephew Ivo come to America. I had heard of the dissatisfaction and unrest with Communism that had been growing throughout the 1970s and 1980s. Was it possible that they would finally be free?

∞ Miljenko "Mike" Grgich

There was a movement for Croatia to split away from Yugoslavia, which had been created after World War I. Many Croatians wanted their country to become independent, as it had been when it was a kingdom in the 12th century. In April 1990, Croatians held their first elections with more than one political party and elected as president Franjo Tuđman, a leader in the movement for Croatian independence.

One month later, in May 1990, something happened that I had never imagined would be possible again: I stepped off an airplane onto the ground in the country of my birth. After thirty-six years, I was home again in Croatia. My heart was filled with happiness.

I went first to Zagreb, the capital city. Although it was far from my home in the south, Zagreb was dear to me as well. Here I had lived for four years as a student, and I still had friends living in Zagreb. I had good memories of these friends and now I was finally able to see them again in person, to laugh and talk and remember the old days.

I was not the only Croatian who returned to their homeland as soon as it was possible after Communism fell. In my hotel in Zagreb there were perhaps a hundred other people who had left Croatia when it was under Communist rule, and now they had come back. There was a special kind of excitement in the air. Still, I could see that the hard rule of Communism and the suppression of free will had drained the country. If you cannot work for yourself, who are you working for? What is there to work for? Without freedom, how can people find happiness and prosperity?

We had left, but now we had returned, and everyone had one question: what can I do to help Croatia? President Tuđman invited me to lunch, and sent a car to my hotel to pick me up. At the Presidential Palace, his wife cooked lunch for us, a good, home-cooked Croatian meal.

So I, Miljenko Grgich, from the village of Desne, sat down to lunch with the President of Croatia. "What can I do for Croatia?" I asked.

"What do you do in America?" President Tuđman asked me.

"In America I make wine," I replied.

"Then perhaps," he said, "you can make wine here too. We need to make better wines."

Yes, I thought, this is something I can do for Croatia. I could bring back to it all the knowledge and experience I had acquired during my years away and help Croatian winemakers move forward and make better quality wines. I began to make plans to build a modern winery in Croatia.

One question had been on my mind for some time: could I finally get my diploma from the University of Zagreb? All those many years ago, I had finished my work, but I had left for Germany without filing my thesis because I knew that once I had officially graduated I would not be permitted to go to Germany.

So, I made inquiries. The answer was a shock to me: there was no record of a Miljenko Grgić attending the University of Zagreb during the years 1950-1954. I had disappeared! This shows what it was like during Communism, and I knew I was lucky I had left when I did; otherwise I might really have disappeared as so many people did, never to be heard of again, in the countries ruled by Communists.

That was a reminder of what life had been like under Communism, but now, all around me, I felt a new spirit in Zagreb that had been absent when I left in 1954. There was optimism and enthusiasm. People had hope for the future.

I traveled south to my home. My brothers and sisters were dead except for my sister Neda but there were still Grgićs in Desne. After the war ended in 1945, my brother Mijo stayed in Desne. The three houses we had owned up on the hills had been destroyed by the Germans. Only the stone walls were left standing. But they were standing. So Mijo repaired the stone house down by the water well and put a roof on it. He had three daughters and a son and it was a great joy for me to be able to meet them when I came home in 1990.

Many people from Desne had immigrated to the United States, even when I was a boy. I remembered that when I was about eight years old, a gentleman by the name of John Medak came back for a visit after fifty years in America. His family and friends in Desne asked him if he saw many changes in the village. He looked at the mountain, Babina Gomila, and pointed to another higher peak behind it. "What is the name of that peak?" he asked. "I forgot."

They replied, "Ježevac." Like everyone else, I was shocked. How could this man, born in Desne, forget the name of Ježevac?

Now a similar thing happened to me when I returned

to Croatia after thirty-six years in America. As I looked at all peaks of the mountains around Desne, I was very surprised because I could only remember half of the names. Then I looked to the lake, Desansko Jezero. In the middle there was a small island where I used to barbecue fish in the early days. To my surprise and that of my sister Neda, I could not remember the name of the island. "It is Goljak," she said.

I told Neda that I could not believe that I forgot the name of the island. A flashback came to my mind of John Medak and how I could not believe that he forgot the name Ježevac. And yet to my surprise, here I was, going through the same experience. When I visited the church in Desne I too could hardly remember the names of the people I met!

In Desne, I climbed the hillside to where our home had been. It was a stone shell now, with grass growing where the fireplace had been. That fireplace was where as a boy I had listened to the adults — my parents, relatives and neighbors — tell their stories.

They were gone now, but I remembered their stories. There was one about a man who comes to a desert, and he wanders through it, wondering who would ever want to live there. He sees a bird singing and asks, "Why do you sing in this place where there is nothing, no water, no plants, no hills, no green?"

The bird says, "My parents lived here before me, and their parents and their parents were all singing here. It is the home of my ancestors, and so it is my home."

Croatia, of course, was not a desert. It is a place of great

After many decades of thinking I would never see my homeland again, here I am in the ruins of my old family home, pointing to the "ognjište", the hearth, where I was born.

natural beauty with its coastline and islands, its mountains, forests and lakes. Still, the greatest part of Croatia is the people who love their country, because it was the home of their parents, grandparents and all of their ancestors.

 The people of Croatia, however, had more hard years ahead of them. When they declared their independence from Yugoslavia, the Serbians, who had dominated Yugoslavia, went to war against the Croatian freedom fighters. They were supported by Serbians who lived within the historical borders of Croatia. The war was long and brutal. When it ended in 1995, thousands of people had been killed and imprisoned. Destruction was great in historic cities like Zagreb and Dubrovnik, and Croatia had been planted with more than two million land mines. But after more than one thousand years, Croatia was again its own country. As it began to rebuild, I went forward with plans for a new winery.

From my Plavac Mali vineyard you can see my winery,
Grgić Vina, in the center of the photo,
with the town of Trstenik just beyond it.

Chapter 18

Grgić Vina

In 1993 my daughter, Violet, and my nephew, Ivo Jeramaz, helped me as I searched throughout Croatia for the site of a new, modern winery that could bring home the technology and expertise I had learned in the course of the years I spent in America.

I was lucky because my search was shortened when my friend Pero Poljanić came up with an idea. He lived in Trstenik, a village on the southern coast of the Pelješac Peninsula, which lies just across the water from my boyhood home. He suggested that I buy an existing two-story stone building previously known as *Karaula* near Trstenik.

Croatia enjoys a long history of winemaking: records show grapes were cultivated here centuries before the birth of Christ. Historically, the Pelješac Peninsula has been known as one of the best wine-growing areas in Croatia. Its most important regions are Dingač and Postup; they are considered the best regions for growing the native Croatian red wine

Miljenko "Mike" Grgich

grape, Plavac Mali.

In the late 19th century the phylloxera epidemic destroyed most of the vineyards in Europe, especially in France and Italy, and the result was a severe shortage of both grapes and wine. Trstenik became an important port from which wines produced in Dingač and Postup were exported to Italy and the rest of Europe.

I once read that a visit to Pelješac peninsula without visiting its vineyards and tasting its wines is like going to Paris without seeing the "Mona Lisa." Today, the Pelješac peninsula is renowned for its domestic wines and food. Farmers are well educated here, much more than in other regions in Croatia.

Trstenik, with a population of about 106 inhabitants, is approximately two hours north by car from the historic walled city, Dubrovnik, in the southern Dalmatian wine region. Trstenik is considered one of the most beautiful villages on the Croatian coast. The water of the Adriatic Sea is crystal clear and has a wealth of fish and underwater life.

The *Karaula* was a government-owned building that had been constructed sometime in the 1940s with stone from Korčula, a nearby island. It had been the site of a military base that served as a lookout point over the Adriatic Sea to protect the Croatian coast from enemy invasion. Eventually it was converted into a thirty-two-room vacation resort for the government employees of an aircraft factory in Mostar.

My friend Pero and another friend, Ivo Katavić, a lawyer in Zagreb, helped me throughout the three-year process of clearing the title and finally purchasing *Karaula*, as well as obtaining approval of the renovation plans and a permit to open a winery.

We began work to convert the facility into a winery, which, in my view, was a far better use for this beautiful place. Srećko Jeramaz, my nephew-in-law and Ivo Jeramaz's father, was instrumental in supervising and ensuring that the renovation was completed.

It was a miracle that I was able to find another Paradise in Croatia!

The Dingač wine-growing region, part of the larger Coastal (Primorska) Region, was the first protected Croatian wine region, established in 1961. It faces the southwestern slope of the Zabrada Mountains and lies between Trstenik and the village of Podobuče.

The land in both Dingač and Postup is rugged karst, a landscape formed from broken down rocks like limestone and dolomite, with little topsoil. These locations have a long history of producing the highest quality of Plavac Mali grapes because of their unique positions. Vines are planted on very steep slopes facing the Adriatic Sea, giving the vines the most important elements for growing fine wine grapes: the reflection of the blue sea below and the white mountains above gives them even more exposure to sunlight than they would ordinarily get. Grapes don't like wet feet, so the gravelly soil is ideal because it allows good drainage, and, along with moderate rainfall, helps produce the best grapes.

Due to the steep terrain the cultivation has always had to be done by hand. The rows of planted vines are so narrow and steep that machines are unable to go in between them.

Dingač is not very accessible and for centuries the grape growers of the town of Potomje had to travel on donkeys and other beasts of burden to cultivate the vineyards. This was tedious and not very efficient for the farmers, so in the early 1970s the grape growers of the area gathered their money and built a one-lane tunnel through the mountain. Construction was finished in 1973. Passing through the tunnel facilitated the transportation of grapes from Dingač directly to the wineries. This replaced the old system of using donkeys to carry harvested grapes over the 400-meter-high pass of the mountain.

There is an extremely narrow one-lane rural road that runs the length of the peninsula. When I was in Croatia in May 2010, my friend Maria and I drove along this road. It was quite an experience! On the left side were mountains where vineyards were being developed and on the right side was the precipice of Dingač with the Adriatic Sea at the tip. At one point I asked Maria to stop.

I got off and walked towards the Dingač side, and Maria took my picture with the 45-degree slope of Dingač and the Adriatic Sea behind me.

I did not know where the road would lead us but I felt strongly that we would end up in Trstenik. We kept driving and the adventure continued. The narrow road eventually led us through the cemetery on the south side of steep Cucin Mountain, which overlooks Trstenik. We came out into the beautiful pebble beach that borders the town. Following that short seaside road through Trstenik we reached Grgić Vina Winery — and home!

When I began this project, people asked me, "Mike, do you plan to make money with this winery?"

My answer was, "No, but I don't plan to lose money either!"

My life experiences in Croatia had taught me about the devastation of war, and if I wanted one thing, what I wanted most for Croatia, as well as for the rest of the world, was this: no more wars. Instead, I wished that Croatia would focus on a much more pleasurable occupation: making the best quality of wines.

My desire was to elevate the quality of local grape and wine varieties in Croatia and abroad by using the best equipment and best techniques. Croatian wines were already for sale in the United States, but those wines had a European character and were not as expensive as American wines. My goal was to upgrade local varieties and produce world-class wine only from local Croatian grapes.

When we started to plan production, we decided we would make only two wines, a red and a white, from Croatia's best varietals. For the red wine we would make Plavac Mali with grapes from the Dingač and Postup regions. In Croatian, Plavac means "blue" and Mali means "small." Plavac Mali is a red grape that thrives on hard, rocky and dry areas in central and southern Dalmatia. It is resistant to numerous fungal diseases, has hard skin and firm berries, and is high in sugar and moderate in acidity. Our Plavac Mali grapes grow on the mountains of the Pelješac Peninsula in small, steep vineyards that face south towards the Adriatic Sea.

The two wines produced by Grgić Vina:
Pošip and Plavac Mali.

Plavac Mali is part of a remarkable story that I will tell in the next chapter and you will see that it is related to California's Zinfandel grape and the Croatian grape, Crljenak Kaštelanski.

The white wine we decided to make was Pošip, the best white local variety that grows in this part of southern Dalmatia. Pošip grapes are grown in the nearby island Korčula, which in 1967 became the first protected Croatian white wine region.

No one knows the history of the origins of Pošip in Korčula — when it was first planted or where it came from, but it is an indigenous white grape that is the result of a spontaneous crossing of two varieties from Korčula. In 2002, Dr. Edi Maletić and Dr. Ivan Pejić, from the University of Zagreb Faculty of Agriculture, determined through DNA testing that the first wild Pošip, found in the woods in the mid-19th century by Marin Barbaca Tomasić near the town of Smokvica, is the offspring of two other varieties, *Bratkovina* and *Zlatarica*, from the town Blato on Korčula.

Pošip has been grown for centuries in Croatia on several islands and along the Dalmatian coast, where the cool winds of the Adriatic Sea provide the perfect temperatures for white grapes. The wine has a distinctive flavor with a characteristic aroma of dried apricots and figs, and is smooth and balanced, very similar to Chenin Blanc wine in Napa Valley.

We purchased Pošip grapes grown in Čara, a sheltered location in Korčula where high quality grapes are produced. The hand-picked grapes are placed in small bins to avoid bruising and premature crushing, then transferred from Korčula by boat to Orebić, and then driven by truck to the winery in Trstenik.

In 2003 the winery had an opportunity to buy 10,000 square meters of unplanted land in the Postup wine region, close to the winery. Postup, which takes its name from the small village that sits at the center of the region, straddles the Adriatic Sea with views across the Pelješac Channel to the islands of Korčula and Badija, as well as across the Mljet Channel to the islands of Mljet and Lastovo.

The main grape harvested in Postup is Plavac Mali, and, like the grapes from the steeper region of nearby Dingač, the grapes grown here are held in high regard. While the wines from Postup do not approach the robust character typical of Plavac Mali-based wines from Dingač, they are still able to develop a fuller body than those grown in the interior, due to the slope of the vineyards as well as the sunlight reflected from the Adriatic Sea.

The grapes are also considerably easier to harvest than those of Dingač because the slopes are not quite as steep and the transportation infrastructure is more established. Postup was the second Croatian wine region after Dingač to be registered for state protection (today called Protected Geographical Status) in 1967.

We planted the land with Plavac Mali but for experimental purposes we planted thirteen vines of Crljenak Kaštelanski, a grape which, by then, we had been able to prove is genetically the same as the American Zinfandel.

Once again, Srećko Jeramaz helped me by supervising the planting of the vines. Srećko, an engineer and a very precise man, made sure that each row was planted exactly the right way. Today we produce from our own vineyard about five to seven tons of high quality red grapes a year.

Once we decided on what wines we would produce I set to work designing the label for Pošip and Plavac Mali. I envisioned the label as a way of sharing the beauty of Trstenik with the people who would drink the wine, so that they would know a little of the place where it was made.

I asked Michele LeBlanc, a designer in Calistoga, to draw Grgić Vina Winery as it sits on a knoll overlooking the clear blue waters of the Adriatic Sea, with a sailboat in the foreground bearing the Croatian crest. Her beautiful work won a label design competition in the United States.

In preparation for establishing Grgić Vina, I bought stainless steel tanks built in Santa Rosa, California. They were transported to Texas by train and then went on by ship to Croatia. I also bought new French oak barrels for the winery. No one in Croatia had ever used French barrels before.

There was one more thing I wanted to put in Grgić Vina. My winery would not be complete without the grape press that I had bought from Chateau Montelena to take with me when we built Grgich Hills in California. This was the same press that I had used to make the 1972 and 1973 Chardonnays. I also used this press for the first two famous Grgich Hills Chardonnays, the 1977 Sonoma Chardonnay that won the 1980 Great Chicago Showdown, as well as the 1977 Napa Valley Chardonnay that garnered a gold medal in the 1980 Orange County Wine Fair.

The press I used for two of my famous Chardonnays, the 1973 Chateau Montelena and the 1977 Grgich Hills, is now being used at Grgić Vina.

This little old press had been part of my success and now I wanted it to be in my homeland of Croatia, in the new winery in Trstenik.

This little press would bring me more luck, as you will see.

We made our first wines, a 1996 Pošip and a 1996 Plavac Mali, using my old press from America. In October 1999 "Croatia Month" was celebrated in the United Nations delegates' dining room in New York. It was a month-long Food and Wine Festival where Croatian dishes and wines were featured. A commission in Zagreb selected the 1997 Grgić Vina Pošip and 1997 Plavac Mali to be served at the United Nations to represent the Croatian wine industry and a chef was flown in from Zagreb to pair his cuisine with Grgić Vina wines.

When I entered the United Nations Headquarters in New York, twenty-eight journalists were waiting for me along with my wines that would be served to dignitaries and representatives of member states from the five continents. I could hardly believe that forty-five years after I had left my homeland, I was setting foot in the organization that gave me a chance to flee Communism and try my luck in the free world. It was one of the few occasions when I forgot that I was a short, small man because I felt, as I had learned to say in America, "ten feet tall!" Our winery was on the road to success.

Today, we manage the operation of Grgić Vina from the Napa Valley. In Croatia, Krešo Vučković is the winemaker and manager, assisted by his wife Dražena. Conto, an accounting firm in nearby Metković, is in charge of our books, and Jelica Jeramaz, Srećko's wife and Ivo's mother, oversees everything that goes on.

Grgić Vina produces 3,000 to 4,000 cases of wine a year, about half of which is Pošip and the other half Plavac Mali. Krešo, our manager, regularly visits the vineyards that supply us to ensure the production of high quality grapes. The winery buys grapes from the best grape growers of Plavac Mali in Pelješac Peninsula and Pošip in Korčula. In the village of Trstenik we buy grapes from top farmers such as Pero Poljanić, his cousin Mate Poljanić and Ivo Cibilić, who is Trstenik's port director and owns the biggest vineyard in the region.

Many of our fans have come from America to taste the wines of Grgić Vina and to see the beauty of its natural setting. A gravel driveway leads up to Grgić Vina, a simple white stone building on a narrow rocky promontory overlooking the Adriatic Sea, surrounded by a grove of fragrant cypress trees. Beyond these trees, the Plavac Mali vines grow amidst wild herbs, holding onto the rocky mountainsides that descend to the sea. Entering the tasting room, visitors hear the traditional Croatian greeting: "Dobro došli u vinariju Grgić!", which means "Welcome to Grgić winery!" I think my Papa would be proud to see that the Grgić name and the family tradition of making wine are carried on in our native land of Croatia.

As we worked to open the new Grgić Vina winery, I received some surprising but good news. With the Communists gone and Croatia now a free country, the Office of the Registrar at the University of Zagreb informed me that they had found the records of Miljenko Grgić who had completed all of the course work for a degree in enology and viticulture. He had only to turn in his thesis to receive his diploma. This news filled me with such joy and a deep sense of fulfillment that I felt like dancing!

So it happened that finally on June 13, 1997, at the age of seventy-four, I was able to take part in the graduation ceremony at the University of Zagreb. I was quite a bit older than the other students receiving their diplomas and I walked a bit slower than they did, but I believe my smile and joy was just as big, if not bigger. It was a proud moment among many in my life and one more miracle for me.

THE VIEW OF TRSTENIK FROM MY APARTMENT OVER GRGIĆ VINA IN CROATIA.

This Crljenak vine found by Professor Edi Maletić in Kaštel Novi on Sept. 7, 2000, was proven, through DNA testing, to be the original Zinfandel.

Chapter 19

The Mystery of Zinfandel

My return to Croatia in 1990 made it possible for me to look for an answer to a question that had been puzzling me since my first night in the Napa Valley in 1958: what was the origin of the Zinfandel grape?

That night as I walked to the lonely cabin that would be my home in this new world, I noticed the grapevines growing in Lee Stewart's Souverain vineyards. The canes, leaves, clusters, the color and size of the berries were all familiar to me. It came to my mind how much they resembled the Plavac Mali grapevines I had come to know on my father's vineyard in Desne. He had grown a mixture of many varietals of grapes, and I could remember and recognize each one by heart. Now, looking at these grapes, I felt like I had found an old friend. I was not alone in America. Had I come home to the same grapevines I had left behind in Croatia?

"What is this grape?" I asked Mr. Lee Stewart. I was told it was Zinfandel, a popular variety that was widely planted in

⁌ Miljenko "Mike" Grgich

California. "Where had this Zinfandel come from?" I asked. To my surprise, no one knew. Everyone could tell you that Chardonnay and Cabernet Sauvignon, the most well known grapes in the Napa Valley, had come from France, and Riesling had come from Germany. But Zinfandel? It was a mystery. I got a book and read similar answers: that the roots of Cabernet Sauvignon came from France, Riesling from Germany, and that the roots of Zinfandel were unknown. Deep inside me I was almost certain that the vines surrounding me at Souverain were the same as the one in the old country. However, I was a poor immigrant who did not know anyone and hardly spoke English. Who would believe me if I told them that I knew that the roots of Zinfandel could be found in Croatia? I kept the knowledge to myself and told myself that one day I would be able to help someone trace the roots of Zinfandel in Croatia.

At a Zinfandel symposium at Sutter Home Winery in St. Helena, I listened to a discussion on how Zinfandel might have gotten to America. There were many theories. Many thought that Zinfandel vines had arrived in the mid-19th century with Count Agoston Haraszthy of Hungary, a colorful adventurer who came to America in the 1840s and worked at many jobs and projects as he made his way across the country to California. He had a great interest in wine and arrived in Sonoma, where he built California's first premium winery, Buena Vista Winery, in 1856. He is often referred to as the "Father of the Wine Industry in California." (The poor man later met an untimely end in Nicaragua, where he was eaten by a crocodile.)

It is possible that Haraszthy brought Zinfandel vines to California, although he was not the first to bring them to

America. The grape has been identified as growing on the East Coast for years before his arrival. Some thought it had come from Vienna, and some thought Italian monks had brought it to America. During this time, Dalmatia, Croatia, was a part of the Kingdom of Hungary. There were records that Croatians had owned vineyards and wineries in California since the 1850s. I thought it might have been Haraszthy who brought Zinfandel to California, or it might have been Croatians who brought it along with their winegrowing expertise from Dalmatia to California during the Gold Rush — from the shores of the Adriatic Sea to the shores of the Pacific Ocean.

As time passed, I found several articles that mentioned the similarity of Zinfandel and Plavac Mali. After Dr. Jerry Seps, of Storybook Mountain Winery in Napa Valley, visited Croatia, he wrote an article suggesting the origin of Zinfandel might be Croatia. Dr. Olmo of UC Davis had received samples of Plavac Mali from Croatia. He did not, however, agree that they were the same as Zinfandel.

Still I had it in my mind that Zinfandel had come from Croatia, but it was not a question that I could answer for many years. When I returned to Croatia in 1990, I looked at the Plavac Mali vines, and I saw that I was not mistaken: they looked the same.

On my next trip to Croatia, in 1993, I brought with me clusters of grapes, leaves and canes from Napa Valley Zinfandel vines to compare. I could see only similarities. I was convinced at the time that they were the same grape.

On that trip I found a book titled *Zinfandel, Primitivo, and*

Plavac Mali, written by a Croatian scientist, Dr. Peter Males. He believed these three grapes were different clones of the same variety.

I had heard that Dr. Carole Meredith, a grape geneticist at UC Davis, had traced the origins of several European grape varietals through DNA testing. I invited her to come to my house in Yountville, where I showed her Dr. Males' book. She was interested so I translated it into English for her. This intrigued her and sparked her desire to travel to Croatia in 1998 to see if she could discover an answer to the puzzle of Zinfandel's origins. She accepted my offer to stay in my winery in Trstenik while searching for the roots of Zinfandel. Dr. Meredith traveled to Croatia with her research assistant, Jasenka Piljac Žegarac, who happened to be Croatian and was able to serve as interpreter. Dr. Meredith told me that on seeing a vineyard of Plavac Mali in Pelješac her first thought was, "What a lot of Zinfandel!"

She brought back samples of 150 Plavac Mali vines to test in laboratories at Davis to see if they were Zinfandel; however, they only proved to be close relatives of Zinfandel.

It was left to two professors from the University of Zagreb, Professors Ivan Pejić and Edi Maletić, who had done research on Pošip, to continue the search for the origin of Zinfandel. On September 7, 2000, near Split in Kaštel Novi, Prof. Maletić found an old vine called Crljenak Kaštelanski. He sent samples to Dr. Meredith at Davis for DNA analysis. She utilized eight different tests to analyze the leaves of this Croatian Zinfandel and all proved that it was the same as Zinfandel found in California.

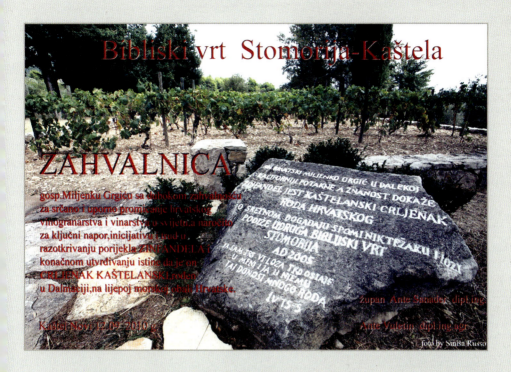

This stone plaque honors my efforts to prove that Zinfandel originated in Croatia. It is located in the "Biblical Garden" by Kaštel Novi, close to where the original Zinfandel/Crljenak vine was found.

Milka Barišić's film "Dossier Zinfandel" was awarded the "Prix Science-Culture" at the Oenovideo International Grape and Wine Film Festival in 2014.

They subsequently found that Crljenak has many offspring in Croatia, one of which is Plavac Mali.

Success! The conclusion of the debate was that the origin of California Zinfandel had been found in Croatia.

I brought Yountville Mayor Mary Lou Holt to Kaštel Novi, where she signed a Sister City agreement, and today there is an inscription on a stone near where the original Zinfandel vines were found that reads, "Miljenko Grgić in faraway California noticed and science proved that the roots of Zinfandel are in Croatia."

After 55 years of guessing, searching, analyzing and testing, professors Maletić and Pejić from the University of Zagreb felt that this important discovery, that the homeland of Zinfandel is Croatia, needed to be documented. So in 2009 they contacted the Croatian radio and television company HRT to ask them to assist, and a documentary film was finally produced by director Milka Barišić.

Dossier Zinfandel premiered at the Zagreb Wine Gourmet Weekend on April 19-20, 2013 and was screened at the third Napa Valley Film Festival in November 2013. In addition, the organizers of Oenovideo International Grape and Wine Film Festival in France asked Barišić to submit the documentary as an entry, and *Dossier Zinfandel* was chosen from among 150 entries to be screened in the 2014 Oenovideo Film Festival. The documentary was awarded the Prix Science-Culture, and Milka Barišić received the award in the French Senate at the Luxembourg Palace in Paris in September 2014. Grgich Hills Estate bought the rights to sell the DVD of *Dossier Zinfandel* in the United States.

Who was the person who first planted Croatian Zinfandel vines in California? This, we will never know. It was an unknown early immigrant who brought to California winemaking traditions, expertise, heritage — and cuttings from a noble Croatian grapevine. But I am proud to have played a part in discovering this connection between Croatia and California.

Why does it matter? For one thing, it shows how strong the winemaking tradition of Croatia is, and also how — although a person may arrive as a newcomer — a refugee with only thirty-two dollars — he might bring more than anyone would imagine.

Although an immigrant may find a new home in a foreign country, he or she will never forget their homeland. This love of homeland is shown, I think, in a poem I found that was written by the famous Croatian writer, August Šenoa. It was published in the *Zagreb Times* newspaper in Croatia in 1862.

A Glass Full of Miracles

Here is its English translation, attributed to Adam S. Eterovich:

CALIFORNIA GOLD, CROATIAN WINE
BY AUGUST ŠENOA

God has blessed California with gold;
Gold has exalted the land far and wide;
Its rivers and brooks roll treasures untold,
Its rocks conceal gold veins in their inside.
But from whatever you have had your fill
You no more derive any joyous thrill.
When it is far, however, what a change!
The gold that leaves its native land, and sails
The ocean to Europe — is it not strange?
May a fine day roll on Austrian rails.
Well, Austrian? Gold? But where is it? Where?
My brothers, in museums. Look it up there.
And we, the gentle souls, think it meet
To be content with a sheer paper sheet.
The country of Croatia overflows with wine,
Its drops more precious than gold, crystalline clear:
God Himself has consecrated our vine,
Its fame expanding world-wide, far and near,
One cannot be a prophet in his land,
Sometimes we may not drink as manners demand.
When far and away, however — what a change!

∽ Miljenko "Mike" Grgich

Whenever leaving your home for some time,
You prize Croatian wine — is it not strange?
You miss it under a foreign clime.
And while I drink that wishy-washy beer,
I often brush away a painful tear.
Then I remember you, my charming home,
Your fiery wine, opulent, flavorsome,
With life in it and real love beside,
With heaven in it and thunderous song.
With olden glory and national pride,
With courage and concept lucid and strong;
Sure cure for old age, bright sunshine for youth,
Proof our hospitality tells the truth.
And you, my brothers in Croatian parts,
Keep on dancing, sing from your fullest hearts;
Our wine is foaming, see it sparkle, my dear,
Let jokes be cut — let everybody cheer,
Propose a toast to too many a son
Who lacks our wine beneath a foreign sun:
Drink moderately to keep yourselves alert
Lest enemies should plan an assault;
Drink boldly to be able to avert
From new-glory-bearing vines any fault;
Drink modestly this divine, fierce gift;
Drink wisely, Mirza teaches, foster thrift.

— *Zagreb Times*, 1862 Croatia

Dr. Carole Meredith finally was able to prove through DNA testing that the original Zinfandel found in California actually originated in my homeland, Croatia.

Heidi Kuhn, founder of Roots of Peace, presents me with their first "Global Citizen Award" in 2007 on board the ocean liner Queen Elizabeth 2. I shared the honor with Queen Noor of Jordan.

CHAPTER 20

THE ROOTS OF PEACE

*M*Y LIFE EXPERIENCES HAVE MADE A "peacenik" of me. When you have lived through the misery and fear of a war fought in your own country, you know that there is nothing more important you can do than to try to prevent it from happening again, and to help heal the wounds a war inflicts. Croatia's War of Independence from 1991 to 1995 had left destruction that could be seen throughout the country, but invisible scars remained in the form of land mines. Estimates are that approximately two million mines had been planted in fields and forests, near schools and hospitals and along roads. There were no plans or records as to where they were laid. Although the war was over, they remained hidden in the ground, waiting to be detonated unexpectedly. Children, farmers, and other innocent people were killed or maimed when they unknowingly stepped on one. Those who survived suffered terrible injuries and amputations. How could a country recover from a war if the people could not return to work in their fields and grow food? As long as the mines remained, so did the terror and evil of war.

Heidi Kuhn, founder and CEO of Roots of Peace, is a cancer survivor who was inspired by the work of Diana, Princess of Wales, a supporter of the International Campaign to Ban Landmines. After the death of Princess Diana in 1997, Heidi decided to continue the work and founded an organization called Roots of Peace, based in her native Marin County, a neighbor of Napa. The mission of Roots of Peace is "to rid the world of land mines by transforming minefields into thriving farmland, literally turning 'Mines to Vines'."

Heidi knew that Croatia, with its terrible legacy of the Balkan War, was a country where her organization could do much good. It would be the first project of her organization.

Removing mines is complicated, costly and dangerous; it requires careful training. Although it costs as little as three to thirty dollars to plant a land mine, it takes thousands of dollars to remove them and return the land to a state where it is safe to plant and grow crops.

Heidi sought the support of the United States Department of State and individual donors. She came to Napa Valley to seek the assistance of vintners who were willing to help her cause. We met when she attended a Grgich Hills Winemaker Dinner in Rutherford in 1998. She told me that she had heard about a Croatian who owned a winery in Napa.

Heidi shared with me the mission of Roots of Peace and how she planned to achieve her goal. I felt fortunate that I had been able to leave Communism in Croatia and achieve my dream of owning a winery in the Napa Valley. I always wanted to share my success with my countrymen and I felt that supporting Roots of Peace would be a good way to do that. I would be able to help clear land mine-infested areas in my homeland. The organization's model of demine-replant-rebuild would return the land to the farmers, allowing them to plant grapevines and make wine, just like their ancestors did.

After meeting Heidi Kuhn at our Yountville home, my daughter Violet traveled with her to Washington, D.C. to meet with Secretary of State Madeleine Albright. They presented Secretary Albright with a gift, a grapevine symbolizing the change they wished to create. Afterward, they joined the Secretary at a dinner honoring nineteen public and private partnerships that were determined to rid the world of land mines by the year 2010.

Heidi worked with Jim Lawrence in the U.S. State Department's Office of Humanitarian Demining programs to organize a visit to Croatia and the village of Dragalić, in the region of Slavonia, the site of her first demining project. She worked with the Croatian Government, the Croatian Mine Action Center and local citizens to find land for growing wheat and grapes. This would give people bread and wine, to share as they do during Mass — Croatia is mostly Roman Catholic. Sharing bread and wine gives people hope and fosters good will.

In May 2000, I traveled to Zagreb, Croatia with other vintners to attend an event called Vino Vitae — Wine is Life. Heidi Kuhn flew to Zagreb with her daughter Kyleigh, who was then 13 years old, because she wanted to see first-hand the war-torn lands of Croatia and felt that it was important that her daughter see this as well.

Before we departed from Zagreb, I handed Heidi a hand-wrapped grapevine from my vineyard in Trstenik as a symbol of planting the "roots of peace" in Dragalić.

The office of the American Ambassador to Croatia arranged and provided land transportation for the Roots of Peace delegation. I led the group to Dragalić that was composed of Heidi and Kyleigh Kuhn, and a delegation from the U.S. Department of State Office of Weapons Removal and Abatement.

When we arrived in Dragalić, the townspeople were happy to see the American delegation, and more so because they saw that a Croatian was with them. Their faces beamed with joy and hope for their future and that of their children.

We wanted to plant the grapevine I had given Heidi in Dragalić, but the United Nations deminers in the area did not allow us to walk through because clearance had not yet been granted. Heidi ended up planting the vine on Mother's Day 2000, in Medjugorje, at the site where it is said that Our Blessed Mother Mary had appeared to three Croatian children. The delegation proceeded to Bibinje, Čista Mala, Čista Velika, Ilok and Karlovač, while I returned to Trstenik.

As the mines came out of the ground, vines went in. In Dragalić, which lies inland, the replanted vines were mostly white wine grapes such as Gewürztraminer, Chardonnay, Riesling and Sauvignon Blanc. Further south in the Dalmatian coast near Zadar, red wine grapes such as Cabernet Sauvignon,

Merlot and Plavac Mali were replanted.

I was able to travel to Dragalić with Heidi to see the transformation slowly but surely taking place. With each grapevine, I felt that hope was planted too.

Meanwhile, back in Napa, we continued to raise money for the work of Roots of Peace. On May 19, 2001, to celebrate the 25th anniversary of the 1976 Judgment of Paris Tasting, Grgich Hills, with the help of my good friend Oscar Rhodes, founder and publisher of the *Yountville Sun* newspaper, organized a wine and food tasting during the day, followed that evening by a gala dinner and silent auction at Domaine Chandon in Yountville. Oscar invited nineteen restaurants while I was able to gather thirty-one wineries to participate, and over 800 people attended.

The event was a huge success and raised $64,000 for Roots of Peace. The funds were matched by both the International Trust Fund and the Croatian Mine Action Center, bringing a total of $192,000 to demine and replant minefields in Croatia.

After the auction, Heidi went to the United Nations to meet with Gillian Martin Sorensen, the Assistant Secretary-General for External Relations in the office of Secretary-General Kofi Annan. Roots of Peace had been chosen as one of four models of a private sector success in zones of conflict, and it was hoped that she could apply the same efforts that had worked well in Croatia to other regions in the world.

On June 18, 2001, at the Rotary Club of San Rafael, I felt honored and privileged when Rotary District Governor Eric Zorr presented me with the Paul Harris Fellowship Award for my "...leadership role in raising land mine awareness and for taking direct action by raising $64,000 for humanitarian demining" in my homeland.

I was elated when the Rotary Club of San Rafael, California, established a Sister City relationship with the Rotary Club of Zadar, Croatia.

The Roots of Peace work continued to rid Croatia of the "seeds of terror" in places like Bibinje, Karlovac, Čista Mala, Čista Velika and Ilok. My personal donation of $50,000 was matched by the International Trust Fund of the U.S. Department of State and used to demine-replant-rebuild Bašćica, which means "Little Garden" in Croatian.

The Rotary Club of San Francisco, Rotary Club of Zadar and the University of Zadar all joined forces to replace "...the scourge of landmines with bountiful vineyards" in Bašćica. Twenty-five thousand vines and 12,500 apple trees have been planted in this little garden to truly transform Bašćica into a little garden.

Adjacent to this site is the demonstration field of the University of Zadar. There, different grape varietals are planted, benefiting students of enology and viticulture — Croatia's future winemakers. I was deeply moved when, in 2010, I was presented with a bottle of the first vintage of wine produced in the area I helped demine, and my heart leaped with joy when Heidi Kuhn informed me that a stone monument would be erected in the little garden in honor of the donations I have made over the years to support the mission and programs of Roots of Peace in Croatia. "Roots of Peace Garden Dedicated to Miljenko 'Mike' Grgich" will be carved in the same Croatian white stone that was used to build the United States White House in Washington, D.C.

April 30, 2007 was a beautiful spring day in New York City, made even more magical when in front of me I saw the Cunard Line's luxury ocean liner, the Queen Elizabeth 2, known as the QE2. I was to board the ship to attend a reception where Grgich Hills wines would be served at a lunch to kick off the "Roots of Peace — Cruise for Peace," a transatlantic voyage from New York to Southampton, England.

I wasn't the only special guest on this voyage. After the luncheon, Heidi Kuhn invited Her Majesty Queen Noor of Jordan and me to the stage. On behalf of Roots of Peace, Heidi presented us with the first Roots of Peace Global Citizen Award for our efforts to help rid the world of landmines.

It was a great privilege for me to share the honor of being a Global Citizen with Queen Noor, an American who had married the King of Jordan and also believed in the work of Roots of Peace. I was overwhelmed to be the co-recipient of such an award with a reigning queen, especially because it was in the presence of three hundred Croatians who had come to share my joy.

In 2008, on the seventh anniversary of the September 11, 2001 terrorist attacks in New York, Heidi Kuhn joined me in tossing the first coins in the Peace Fountain we had constructed at the entrance of Grgich Hills Estate. Since that day visitors to the winery can toss coins into the Peace Fountain; these are collected and donated to Roots of Peace.

◦ Miljenko "Mike" Grgich

To me, it shows that every contribution, however small, helps a good cause; everyone can help. People ask me, is it a wishing fountain? Can they make a wish when they throw in their coin? Of course everybody is welcome to make a wish. And my own wish is for peace and for the roots of peace to spread throughout the world. Today the work continues to remove land mines from countries where wars have been fought, helping return the land to its best purpose, to grow crops and feed people — and to make wine.

Heidi's ideas really took root, you might say. Today Roots of Peace has grown large enough to help other countries around the world, including Afghanistan, Vietnam, Cambodia, and Israel and the Gaza Strip. But more than twenty years after the war ended in Croatia, not all of the land mines have been found and removed. This is the terrible legacy of war.

Queen Noor of Jordan and I aboard the QE2 after the awards. She is even more gracious and lovely in person!

This documentary movie about my life premiered at the Napa Valley Film Festival in 2012 and won the Grand Jury Special Award at the Oenovideo International Grape and Wine Film Festival in France in 2013. I won — again — in Paris!

Chapter 21

Like the Old Vines

*J*anuary 1, 2000: A new century began, and I, at seventy-seven years old, had a lifetime of memories and miracles. What would I do next?

The wine industry in the Napa Valley was changing. Hundreds of new wineries had opened; everywhere people were planting vineyards in what had been pastures and orchards. They were building mansions on the hillsides, and limousines mixed with tractors and pickup trucks on the roads. The Napa Valley had become famous and rich.

Many of the new wineries were built in the grand chateau style that made our modest Grgich Hills winery look humble indeed, yet Austin Hills and I were happy with what we had achieved. We had loyal customers who traveled across the country to come to our Wine Club parties and new customers who visited our winery or bought our wines in faraway places.

At Grgich Hills we kept to our policy of sure and steady

growth. I did not want to grow so big that I could not watch over the quality of every bottle of wine, and I did not want to go into debt for the sake of grandeur. Grgich Hills had achieved an independence that I could hardly have imagined when I dreamed of owning a small patch of land that I could call my own.

As my daughter Violet and my nephew Ivo continued to grow in their roles at Grgich Hills and as I approached my 80th birthday, my attention turned to the property in Calistoga that I had bought in 1997, with its old Zinfandel vines planted in 1889. I felt that this property would be the perfect location for my last house.

Building my house overlooking Miljenko's Vineyard turned out to be a bigger project — and a bigger house — than I had anticipated. It involved getting permits and approval to build on a hillside. This bureaucratic process, however, did not compare with the pressure I had gone through back in 1977 to obtain the permits and meet the requirements to build the winery in a short period of time.

When the construction of the house was finished in 2001, it turned out to be a grand house. I wondered what was I going to do in such a big house full of machines: a dishwasher, washing machine, dryer, fax machine, printer, central heating and air conditioning and countless bulbs. So many things could break down.

The story of my life is one of luck making repeated visits. Luck struck again when I saw Maria Luisa Moreno Reyes in 2002 at a dinner for Roots of Peace at the United Nations in

New York. I saw her that evening and I don't think she noticed me but I didn't forget her. She was working for the United Nations in the Executive Office of the Secretary-General. Today, she helps me in so many ways, right down to helping me write this book.

This new house was quite a change from the one-room cabin at Souverain on Howell Mountain where I'd stayed when I first arrived at Lee Stewart's almost fifty years earlier. And it was certainly different from the humble little house with the crooked floor that I'd bought for $8,500 in St. Helena. Yet, I love my dream home overlooking Miljenko's Vineyard. The windows open to a view that has always filled me with happiness, and alongside the house I have a vegetable garden and a variety of fruit trees: apples, figs, plums, pears, and a white peach tree, whose fruit I eagerly wait for each spring. When I walk through the vineyards or out to my garden to pick tomatoes or zucchini, I have a connection with all the stages of my life, going all the way back to my parents and family in the old country. All the places I have lived and worked, all the things I have learned and done have brought me here to this hillside where I have my peaceful views of the mountain and my grapevines.

I recently realized that I have become an old-timer in the Napa Valley, one of the "pioneers" who rebuilt the wine industry that had been asleep for so many years after Prohibition. So many of my friends and colleagues from those early days are gone now. Lee Stewart passed away in 1986; André Tchelistcheff in 1994. We lost Brother Timothy in 2004 and Robert Mondavi in 2008.

∽ Miljenko "Mike" Grgich

The old days, when the Napa Valley Vintners met at lunches to discuss their wines and to hear guest speakers from UC Davis and the Technical Group exchanged ideas over dinners at Copper Chimney, have disappeared. Today, with so many new vintners and winemakers, there isn't a restaurant big enough that will accommodate all of them. More and more winemakers are going their own way.

One thing that does unite grape growers, however, is the increasing awareness of how fragile and precious our valley is. When I arrived in the Napa Valley, chemicals were commonly used; for every disease, the solution was to spray chemicals on the grapevines. At Grgich Hills, I always had in my mind to farm the way my father did, without pesticides, fungicides or artificial fertilizers. He didn't use chemicals, and we could drink the wine with pleasure and without care. I like the natural way my father produced wine in the old country.

Ivo led the way in establishing our organic farming practices, and for a time he was also intrigued with the philosophy of Biodynamic farming. This is an interesting philosophy, part mystical and part practical. I agreed that he could try Biodynamic farming, but ultimately it did not have enough science to appeal to me. The wines were not better but cost more. Each person making wine has to discover his or her own best way to farm and make wines.

I have always known that great wines begin in the vineyards. In 2006 all 366 acres of Grgich Hills vineyards were certified organic. This was better for the land, and therefore better for the grapes. That same year we installed solar panels and Grgich Hills became powered by the sun. In 2007, recognizing that we grew all of our grapes on our own vineyards, we changed the winery name to Grgich Hills Estate. All of these changes gave us a new motto for our wines: "From our vineyard to your glass, naturally."

I now walk more slowly with a cane through the vineyards, smelling and tasting my grapes, something that has given me great joy and fulfillment all my life. Instead of finding the cane a nuisance I feel that it is an asset because I jokingly say, "A winemaker needs three legs — one leg in the vineyard, one in the winery and a third leg in the market. I was born with only two legs but now this cane is my third leg!"

When the cold weather of winter comes I can feel it in my bones. I had never done well in the cold so in my mid-80s I began to go south after Thanksgiving, to warm my bones in the desert sun of La Quinta in Coachella Valley in Southern California.

But whether I am in La Quinta or Napa I still like to work every day. I want to be there to guide this winery that is my American dream come true and to make sure that it will be in good order for those who will come after me, not just my daughter and nephew, but now my grandson, Noel, born in 2005 after Violet married a fellow musician, Colin Shipman.

Although it is not easy to grow old and feel your body grow weaker, one of the benefits is being able to witness recognition for your life's work. For me, one of my most significant honors came when I was inducted into the Vintners Hall of Fame on March 7, 2008. The historic Greystone

I was greatly honored to be inducted into the Vintners Hall of Fame in 2008.

building where I once worked for the Christian Brothers had become the western campus of the Culinary Institute of America, but the Barrel Room, which is lined with giant old redwood barrels that were once used to make wines, has become the Hall of Fame, commemorating those who helped create California's wine industry. On the old barrels, you'll find brass plaques with images of Robert Mondavi, André Tchelistcheff, Brother Timothy and many more. Their stories tell the story of wine in California, and I am honored to be among them.

An unexpected project arose when Milka Barišić, a film director and writer at HRT Radiotelevision in Zagreb, traveled to Napa Valley to make the film about the roots of Zinfandel. Her interviews with me inspired her to make a documentary about my life, *Kao Stara Loza — Like The Old Vine: The Life Story of Miljenko "Mike" Grgich*. The film premiered in the 2012 Napa Valley Film Festival, and so on November 7, 2012 I found myself sitting in the Cameo Theater in St. Helena to watch a documentary about my life. Can you imagine?

In early 2013 the organizers of the Oenovideo International Grape and Wine Film Festival in France asked that *Kao Stara Loza: Like the Old Vine* be submitted as an entry. It was selected and shown in the medieval city of Carcassonne, France on May 30, 2013, when judges and festivalgoers viewed twenty-six films from fourteen countries.

The documentary was the winner of the Grand Jury's Special Award and on September 27, 2013, Violet flew to Paris to represent me at the award ceremony along with all the winners, when Milka Barišić received the Cep d'Or Trophy in the French Senate at the Palais du Luxembourg.

In my excitement I could not help but tip my beret and thank the jury for picking my documentary. Thirty-seven years after the 1976 Paris Tasting, the French once again declared me, Mike Grgich, a winner! Was the French beret I bought when I was a student in Zagreb a foreshadowing of the victories I would win in Paris — twice?

Another award I was honored to receive was the prestigious Thomas Jefferson Award presented by the Pennsylvania Academy of the Fine Arts during its annual Bacchanal Wine Gala on November 9, 2013 when they celebrated Napa and the historic 1976 Paris Tasting. This award goes to members of the wine industry to honor connections with President Thomas Jefferson and his love of fine wine.

In 1996, on the twentieth anniversary of the Paris Tasting, the Smithsonian Institution in Washington, D.C. commemorated its determination of the importance of American wines by unveiling an exhibit featuring the two winning wines. A bottle of my 1973 Chardonnay and Stag's Leap Wine Cellars 1973 Cabernet Sauvignon have been in the Museum of American History since then.

A few years later, representatives from the Smithsonian Institution National Museum of American History in Washington, D.C. came to my house in Calistoga and carried away five boxes containing my personal items for their historical archives. In November 2012 the Smithsonian inaugurated an exhibition titled "FOOD: Transforming the

American Table 1950-2000." Included in the display were my old beret, the little cardboard suitcase I carried when I left Croatia, my Croatian wine books, and the ebullioscope I brought with me from Croatia.

I was already proud to be a part of American history but the Smithsonian had an even greater surprise in store for me. In 2014, the Institution released the book *History of America in 101 Objects*. The author, Richard Kurin, under-secretary for History, Art and Culture of the Smithsonian Institution, had selected these objects from the Institution's entire collection of 137 million objects, and among them were the two winning wines from the Judgment of Paris! They joined such other objects as Abraham Lincoln's hat, Alexander Graham Bell's telephone and Neil Armstrong's spacesuit.

When asked about my reaction after looking over the list of "101 Objects," I said, "When I was growing up in the little village of Desne in Croatia, I never would have dared to dream that my wine would be in the same book as America's Declaration of Independence, or in the same museum as Nikola Tesla, the famous inventor who is also from Croatia. When I arrived in the United States, I thought I was the luckiest man alive to have my dream come true of making wine in California, but this recognition far exceeds my American dream."

It is a good thing to be recognized for what you have achieved but sometimes I think the greatest honor comes from the people who drink and enjoy my wines. I hear many stories from them; one of the most interesting came in the

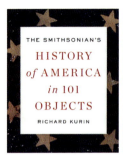   

1973 Chateau Montelena Chardonnay crafted by Miljenko "Mike" Grgich named to Smithsonian's "101 Objects that Made America"

Wine joins Abraham Lincoln's hat, Alexander Graham Bell's telephone and Neil Armstrong's spacesuit.

Rutherford, CA – The 1973 Chateau Montelena Chardonnay crafted by Miljenko "Mike" Grgich that was the champion of the 1976 Paris Tasting is part of the exhibit selected by the Smithsonian Institute as one of "101 Objects That Made America." Chosen from 137 million artifacts in the Smithsonian collection, the Chardonnay is joined by other iconic American objects, such as Abraham Lincoln's hat, Alexander Graham Bell's telephone and Neil Armstrong's spacesuit.

The Smithsonian's *History of America in 101 Objects* chose Julia Child's Kitchen, which includes the 1973 Chateau Montelena Chardonnay crafted by Grgich, in a major exhibition on the revolution in American wine in the second half of the 20th century, and the book features a photo of the winning wine. The author, Richard Kurin, the Smithsonian Institution's Under Secretary for History, Art and Culture, selected objects from the entire collection held by the 19 museums and research centers of the Smithsonian Institution.

Looking over the list of 101 treasures from the Smithsonian's collection, Grgich commented: "When I was growing up in the little village of Desne in Croatia, I never would have dared to dream that the wine I crafted would be in the same book as America's "Declaration of Independence," or in the same museum as Nikola Tesla, the famous inventor who is also from Croatia. When I arrived in the United States, I thought I was the luckiest man alive to have my dream come true of making wine in California, but this recognition far exceeds my American Dream."

Located at 1829 St. Helena Highway (Hwy. 29) in Rutherford, Grgich Hills Estate was founded in 1977 by Vintners Hall of Fame inductee Miljenko "Mike" Grgich and Austin Hills after the 1973 Chateau Montelena Chardonnay that Grgich made outscored the best of France in the now-famous 1976 Paris Tasting that revolutionized the world of wine. Today this iconic winery farms 366 acres naturally, without artificial fertilizers, pesticides or herbicides, and uses its passion and art to handcraft food-friendly, balanced and elegant wines. Mike is assisted by his daughter, Violet Grgich, Vice-President of Operations, and his nephew, Ivo Jeramaz, Vice-President of Vineyards and Production. For more information, visit www.grgich.com.

A Glass Full of Miracles

form of a letter from a lady who wrote to say that many years ago I had signed a bottle of Miljenko's Old Vine Zinfandel for her. She had reluctantly permitted her husband to open the wine so that they could drink it, but there was one condition. They had to keep the empty bottle so that her ashes could be placed in it when she passed away. She and her husband made a special trip to the winery in October 2014 to buy another signed bottle for her husband because she insisted that his ashes have no place in her own bottle! Now that is a compliment!

Here is the secret to longevity:
set yourself on a quest for perfection.

Chapter 22

The Perfect Wine

When I began to write this book, I had it in my mind to call it, "The Search for the Perfect Chardonnay." This was in part because this had been my quest for many years, because Chardonnay has been such an important part of my success, and because one of the questions I am most often asked is: "What is your secret to making wine? How do you make the perfect Chardonnay?"

What can I tell people?

There are technical details that I can share. In the process of making fine wine we pay attention to the minutest details, so every movement must be perfect. Making wine can be compared with making a chain; every chain is made of links. Every link has to be perfect because a chain is only as strong as its weakest link.

It begins with the grapes. Fine wine can only be made from high quality grapes. The time of picking is of utmost importance. A winemaker can only make the best Chardonnay when he has his eyes and mind in his vineyard.

As it nears harvest, he must check and check again the sugar levels in the grapes with a refractometer, and the pH and acid levels by lab analyses. He must taste the berries and inhale their aromas. As grapes mature, their elements — sugar and tannin, pH, color, aroma and acid — all move toward balance. By using analyses as well as smell and taste to find that point of balance, he knows that it is finally time to pick the Chardonnay. The best results are obtained when the grapes are handpicked during the cool night to retain their delicate flavors and aromas, and then immediately pressed to protect the picked grapes from oxidation. Sometimes it helps to add a small amount of SO_2 after picking.

After pressing, the grape juice is moved into a temperature controlled fermentation tank and is chilled to 50 degrees Fahrenheit, where it is allowed to settle. After two days, the sediment has settled to the bottom of the tank and the clear juice on top is racked to another tank and warmed up to about 60 degrees, allowing fermentation to start. Fermentation is started with natural yeast, which is already present on the grape skins, so nothing has to be added. After fermentation starts, the wine is then chilled again down to 50 to 55 degrees, then moved into 60-gallon oak barrels, where it ferments until it is dry and no sugar is left.

Barrels are where the wine ages and matures, receiving small amounts of aromas and extractives from the oak, in moderation, to achieve greater complexity and balance.

After six to eight months in oak, depending on the vintage, Chardonnay is sterile filtered and bottled. Bottles are closed with cork, a natural material allowing the wine to slowly breathe and enabling longevity, and then placed in recycled cardboard case boxes. The cases are moved to what I call the "Honeymoon Suite" for a minimum of one to two years. Why? In the bottle, under anaerobic conditions, a new process starts whereby all the individual elements of the Chardonnay, the fruit, yeast and moderate flavors of oak, marry into a complex and harmonious "bouquet."

You can see that everything is done naturally, using the same methods that my father, Nikola Grgić, practiced in making his wines.

But does this explain how to make great wines? No, much more is needed. We need to utilize science, but having scientific knowledge alone is not enough. To make great wines, we need the artist winemaker.

When I was young I used to hear the elders say that wine, music and song please man's soul. Just as a painter expresses himself through his paintings or a musician through his compositions, the artist winemaker pours his passion, scientific knowledge, and intellectual creativity into a bottle of wine.

My daughter Violet is a musician. I am overwhelmed when I see how her fingers and body motions are balanced as she plays the harpsichord. Music, art and winemaking have this in common — balance. When all the essential elements are in harmony, the results are the highest quality of masterpiece.

∽ Miljenko "Mike" Grgich

We need artist winemakers because making wine is like creating a work of art. A painter can paint hundreds of pictures, but not all of them will necessarily be a true work of art. She must search for the way to make one beautiful picture. A sculptor, making something from a stone, has in mind what he wants to achieve and he has to take his time until he says, "Yes."

This is how a winemaker has to feel about his wines. You must combine knowledge, art, and something more: feelings and soul. You have to put your soul and personality into your wine. The result stands out from the rest, because it reflects your inner soul and individuality. When that is accomplished, then the winemaker too can say, "Yes."

In my life, I have seen great improvements in the quality of wine, but I am often asked now, "Can wines get even better?" I say, of course they can; there's no end to it. The next improvements will come from those who will make small quantities but excellent quality, from the artist winemaker. Only an artist winemaker can make a perfect wine because he makes wine from the heart.

A winemaker who uses both body and mind to excel has to have passion and patience, and often sacrifice. When you plant grapevines, you know it will be four or five years before they are ready to produce grapes. When grapes are harvested, it will be time before the wine can be released. To achieve this requires commitment and dedication.

I will say this too: there is room for many winemakers to make wine. There are a variety of different styles using

The perfect wine? That is for you to decide. If it says "more!!!" as it goes down your throat, then you have found it.

I FEEL LIKE A PROUD FATHER: MOTHER NATURE, WITH A LITTLE HELP FROM ME, PRODUCED THESE BEAUTIFUL CHARDONNAY GRAPES. ALL OF MY SOUL, MY PASSION AND MY ART WILL GO INTO THEM TO CREATE A WINE THAT TRULY COMES FROM MY HEART.

different technologies with different results and each will find its own customer — there is no right one. How do you know what style is best for you? It is when you take a sip of wine, and as it goes down your throat it says, "More!"

So the answer is, there is no sure-proof, scientific, secret formula for making great wines. You don't make wine only with your head and your senses, you make it with your heart. You have to pour your heart and your love into the wine. To me, wines are like children. You have to love and guide them and give to them the richness of your own spirit. Throughout the years I learned how to communicate with my wines, how to nurture them. It is a language that cannot be taught but must be learned by experience.

But finally we must never forget that Mother Nature — some would say God — is the real winemaker. After all, one must work together with Mother Nature to preserve what is best in the grapes, in the vines one has nurtured and watched grow and mature. What God has created is more valuable than what humans can create. This saying best expresses this idea for me: "The soul of fine wine — it's the voice of the earth."

A Glass Full of Miracles

A Multitude of Harvests

Walking with partner Austin Hills in our Rutherford Vineyard.

I'm very excited about our newly released 1984 Fumé Blanc!

I AM STANDING IN THE VINEYARD WHERE CRLJENAK — ZINFANDEL — WAS DISCOVERED, WITH THE VINEYARD'S PROUD OWNER, IVICA RADUNIĆ.

My lifelong friend and wine author Ivo Sokolić visited me at Grgić Vina in 2010.

REPUBLIC OF CROATIA
UNIVERSITY OF ZAGREB
FACULTY OF AGRICULTURE IN ZAGREB

DIPLOMA

ON UNIVERSITY QUALIFICATIONS OF THE SEVENTH (VII/1) GRADE

MILJENKO GRGIĆ

born on April 1, 1923 in Desne, Community of Metković, Republic of Croatia, has completed on June 9, 1997 at the Faculty of Agriculture in Zagreb the program of studies

FRUIT AND WINE-GROWING AND VINICULTURE

in the duration of eight semesters.

The Faculty of Agriculture in Zagreb hereby ascertains that MILJENKO GRGIĆ has passed all necessary examinations and has fulfilled all other regulations pursuant to the program of studies of Fruit and Wine-growing and Viniculture, acquiring university qualifications of the seventh (VII/1) grade and the professional title

**BACHELOR OF AGRICULTURE -
FRUIT AND WINE-GROWING AND VINICULTURE SPECIALIST**

as well as all rights appertaining unto him.

Class: 602-04/97-04/04
Number: 380-71-04-97-65
Zagreb, June 9, 1997

DEAN
Prof. Dr. Sc. FRANJO TOMIĆ

MANY DECADES AFTER LEAVING CROATIA I FINALLY RECEIVED MY DIPLOMA ON JUNE 13, 1997, AT THE RIPE OLD AGE OF 74.

When my assistant Maryanne Wedner came back from a visit in May 1996 to the Smithsonian Institution Museum of American History in Washington D.C. and showed me this picture that she had taken in the museum of the 1973 Chardonnay I had crafted, I was so amazed I nearly fell off my chair! The exhibit was called "History in the News."

CALIFORNIA'S PIONEERS

The modern era of the now thriving California wine industry began in the mid 1960s.
JONATHAN GOODALL goes west and meets the people who made it happen

ANOTHER MEETING OF THE MINDS — CALIFORNIA PIONEERS IN
JUNE 1996. TOP ROW, LEFT TO RIGHT: BERNARD PORTET,
JAMIE & JACK DAVIES. BOTTOM ROW, LEFT TO RIGHT:
DICK GRAFF, ROBERT MONDAVI, PAUL DRAPER, MIKE GRGICH,
CHARLIE WAGNER, AL BROUNSTEIN, DAVE STARE.

Enjoying the mustard in our Yountville vineyard with Violet.

My daughter Violet at her harpsichord.
It's not quite as portable as her accordion!

At my home in Calistoga with my grandnephew Nikola Grgić, who is studying winemaking at the University of Zagreb.

I love to revisit my childhood in Croatia by stomping grapes every year!

My daughter Violet and her husband Colin Shipman at my 90th birthday party serenade me with my favorite songs, "You Are My Sunshine" and "Marijana".

My young grandson Noel reaching for his favorite food — grapes!

My grandson Noel is already an entrepreneur! He sold "little dudes" that he made from the leftover corks at a wine tasting and earned over $58.

My grandson Noel Grgich Shipman with my daughter Violet, toasting me on my 90th birthday with his favorite beverage. Can you guess what it is?

With my longtime friend and assistant Maryanne Wedner and her mother Sue Ruh.

With my friend Maria Luisa Moreno Reyes, stomping grapes at our annual Wine Club Stomp Party.

At the CIA event celebrating my 50 years in Napa Valley with my longtime friend and counsel, Theodore Kolb, and his cousin-in-law Doris Kolb.

I was proud and honored in 2003 to receive the very first Ho'okele' Award for Lifetime Achievement at the Kapalua Wine and Food Festival in Maui, Hawaii, and from such a wonderful and talented person as renowned Master Sommelier Andrea Robinson.

This is my favorite picture of our Blessing of the Grapes, in 1984. You can see the drops of holy water sparkling in the sunlight, like little "miracles".

The ocean is one of my favorite places to enjoy Mother Nature. Here I am chasing my dog Pošip on the beach at Bodega Bay.

I had a very special day with my grandson Noel at the beach.

I'm very happy that Violet decided to follow in my footsteps.

The Grgich and Hills families together at my 90th Birthday Gala in April of 2013.

I received this special Resolution (Members Resolution No. 1817) from the California Legislature on July 7, 2007, in honor of the 30th anniversary of Grgich Hills Estate.

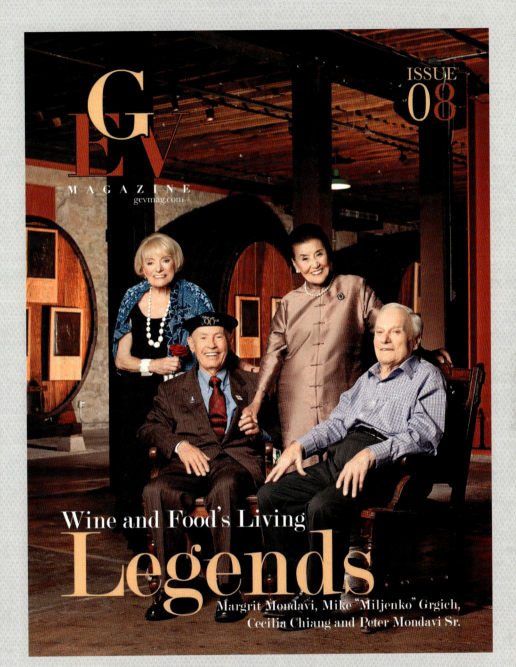

In August of 2008 I celebrated my 50 years in America with a gala at the Culinary Institute of America. Behind me you can see two winning wines from the Paris Tasting. They were auctioned off that night and helped fund a scholarship to the CIA.

CHAPTER 23

MIRACLES

*T*O BE ABLE TO GIVE BACK, I think, is the final link that completes your life. So many people helped me in my quest to realize my dreams and I wanted to reciprocate by helping others.

My work with Roots of Peace was important because I knew I was helping the country of my birth recover from war. I also wanted to do something here in the Napa Valley.

From its beginning in 1981 I supported the Napa Valley Wine Auction (now Auction Napa Valley) because its purpose was to provide healthcare for the farmworkers in the valley — where would we be without them, after all? The proceeds of the Wine Auction became the seeds of establishing Clinic Olé in Napa. It now provides health care for many residents of the valley who would have no other place to go for health care. I continue to support this worthy place with an annual donation.

name for professional wine studies at the CIA.

In March 2014, in partnership with the James Beard Foundation, I established the Miljenko "Mike" Grgich American Dream Scholarship to provide deserving young wine professionals an opportunity to succeed and to honor the adoptive country that has given me so much.

I also wanted to help students in my alma mater, the University of Zagreb in Croatia. In December 2012 it was very satisfying for me to be able to establish a one million dollar Miljenko "Mike" Grgich endowment with the Croatian Scholarship Fund in the United States to provide scholarships for students in the master's degree program majoring in viticulture and enology. I want to help educate the future winegrowers and winemakers of Croatia so that my vision for my homeland to develop a world-class wine industry can be achieved.

The first three recipients of the scholarship, Daniel Božac, Petra Balažić and Marina Šeparovič, interned in northern California wineries during the 2014 harvest. When they had finished their work, they came to meet me in the Grgich Hills Legacy Room on November 18, 2014.

We sat and talked about life and wine, and I shared with them the wisdom from the vineyards that I had learned from my 89 harvests. I told them the lessons I had learned from my own father and about the series of links in crafting fine wine and how each one is important. I shared with them what I have realized are the elements of a happy life: God, friends, family — and wine.

I told them too that my brother Mijo's grandson, Nikola